Discovering Welsh History · Book 2

Wales in the Middle Ages

Catrin Stevens

Oxford University Press 1992

The publishers wish to thank the following
for permission to reproduce copyright material:

front cover: (Dolwyddelan Castle, one of the castles of the Princes of Gwynedd) Cadw; p.7 *top left and right* John Brennan, *bottom left and right* Tapisserie de Bayeux; p.9 *top* Tapisserie de Bayeux, *bottom* Peter Humphries; p.10 Wales Tourist Board; p.12 Cadw; p.13 National Museum of Wales; p.16 National Museum of Wales (Welsh Folk Museum); p.17 *bottom* Cadw, *inset* National Museum of Wales; p.18 *left* Jonathan Parkhouse/the Glamorgan-Gwent Archaeological Trust/Cadw, *right* by permission of The British Library; p.19 Bodleian Library, University of Oxford; pp.20-21 The Glamorgan-Gwent Archaeological Trust; p.22 *left* Marian Delyth, *right* Cadw; p.23 *left* The Board of Trinity College Dublin, *top right* National Library of Ireland, *bottom right* Peter Hope Jones; p.24 National Museum of Wales; p.25 Cadw; p.27 Cadw; p.28 by permission of The British Library; p.30 *left* Andes Press Agency, *right* Clwyd Record Office; p.33 The National Gallery; p.34 Cadw; p.35 *top left* National Library of Ireland, *bottom left and right* Cadw; p.36 Public Record Office; p.37 by permission of The British Library; p.38 *left* Woodmansterne Picture Library, *right* Cardiff City Council; p.39 *top left* Wales Tourist Board, *bottom left* Pontarddulais Male Choir, *top right* Split Second, *bottom right* Cymdeithas yr Iaith Gymraeg; p.40 *left and centre* Richard Avent, *right* The National Library of Wales; p.41 Cadw; p.46 National Library of Wales; p.49 *top* Cadw, *bottom* Magma Designs, Beaumaris; p.50 National Museum of Wales; p.51 Cadw; p.52 *left* Mary Evans Picture Library, *right* British Tourist Authority; p.53 by permission of the British Library; p.54 The Mansell Collection Limited; p.55 Windsor Castle, Royal Library, Her Majesty the Queen; pp.56-57 Marian Delyth; p.58 Wales Tourist Board, *inset* Oxford University Press; p.60 Cadw; p.61 Sonia Halliday Photographs; p.62 Public Record Office; p.63 David and Charles Ltd, Newton Abbot; p.64 Cadw; p.65 by permission of The British Library; p.66 National Library of Wales; p.69 The Mansell Collection Limited; p.70 *top* Cardiff City Council, *bottom* National Museum of Wales; p.71 National Museum of Wales (Welsh Folk Museum); p.75 Bodleian Library, University of Oxford; p.77 by permission of The British Library; p.79 The Clwyd-Powys Archaeological Trust; p.82 by permission of The British Library; p.83 *top right* Marian Delyth, *inset* National Library of Wales; p.84 Lambeth Palace Library; p.86 *top left* Ysgol Dyffryn Nantlle, Penygroes, *bottom left* Oxford University Press; p.87 *bottom left* Dyfed County Council, *bottom right* University of Wales; p.88 The Royal National Eisteddfod of Wales; p.90 by courtesy of the Board of Trustees of the Victoria and Albert Museum; p.91 J. Salmon Limited, Sevenoaks, Kent; p.92 *left* St David's Cathedral, *right* Oxford University Press; p.93 Thomas Lloyd/Royal Commission on Ancient and Historical Monuments in Wales; p.94 *inset* The Landmark Trust, *bottom* Mary Evans Picture Library; p.95 The Royal Collection.

Illustrations by: John Brennan, Gordon Davidson, Nick Harris, Nick Hawken, Richard Hook, Andrew Howat, Margaret Jones, Bernard Long, Chris Molan, Tony Morris, David Palmer and Maggie Silver.

Designer and Art Editor: John Brennan, Oxford
Picture Researcher: Anne E. Williams, Cardiff

Oxford University Press, Walton Street, Oxford OX2 6DP

Oxford   New York   Toronto
Delhi   Bombay   Calcutta   Madras   Karachi
Petaling Jaya   Singapore   Hong Kong   Tokyo
Nairobi   Dar es Salaam   Cape Town
Melbourne   Auckland

and associated companies in
Berlin and *Ibadan*

Oxford is a trade mark of Oxford University Press

ISBN 0 19 917139 4

Typeset by MS Filmsetting Limited, Frome, Somerset
Printed in Hong Kong

Contents

NORMAN CONQUEST 1066-1200

MOTTE AND BAILEY
CASTLES

NORMAN MANORS

EDWARDIAN CONQUEST 1282-1284

EDWARDIAN CASTLES

1284
STATUTE OF RHUDDLAN

EDWARDIAN
BOROUGH TOWNS

THE WELSH STRIKE BACK

1349
THE BLACK DEATH

1372 - OWAIN OF
THE RED HAND

1400
OWAIN GLYN DŴR

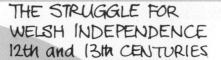

THE STRUGGLE FOR WELSH INDEPENDENCE
12th and 13th CENTURIES

THE NORMAN CHURCH

THE WHITE MONKS

1176 - GERALD THE WELSHMAN and St. DAVIDS

THE AGE OF PRINCES

1282 LLYWELYN II - THE LAST

c. 1220 LLYWELYN I - THE GREAT

Late 12th Century LORD RHYS of DEHEUBARTH

c1450 - THE GOLDEN AGE OF POETRY

1485 - THE BEGINNING OF THE TUDOR AGE

HENRY VII and THE BATTLE OF BOSWORTH

The Normans are Coming

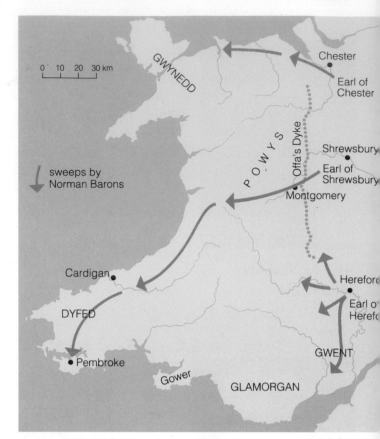

Wales in Medieval times

If you look carefully at the map showing Wales over nine hundred years ago, you can see that the country was divided into a number of kingdoms. Look for Gwynedd, Dyfed, Powys, Glamorgan and Gwent on the map. These are names of Welsh counties today. But the old kingdoms were very different from our modern counties. Each kingdom was ruled by its own king. The King of Powys was as important and as strong as the King of Dyfed or Glamorgan. The kings fought each other regularly.

Although these kings and kingdoms were independent of one another, they still thought that they were all Welsh people living in a country called Wales. They had their own Welsh language, their own Church, laws, heroes, stories, and poetry, and their own history. All these made them different from the Anglo-Saxon people who lived over Offa's Dyke in England.

Every now and then one king would try to become ruler over all the kingdoms and make himself the main king of his country. One such king was Gruffudd ap Llywelyn of Gwynedd. He conquered the whole of Wales before he died in 1063. The Welsh chronicler, who kept an account of the history of this time, called Gruffudd 'the head and shield and defender' of his people. His death must have shaken the whole of Wales.

Then, in 1066, one of the most important events in the history of England took place. Duke William, from Normandy in northern France, sailed across the English channel to conquer England. His army of 7,000 Norman knights and archers defeated King Harold of England at the Battle of Hastings. The Normans were able to defeat the English because

Norman knights fought on horseback and because all their soldiers wore good strong armour. As soon as they could after they won the battle, the Normans built a castle to protect their newly-conquered lands.

Now the Normans were ready to begin their great conquest of the rest of the island of Britain. During the next few years, William the Conqueror's armies swept through almost the whole of England. They built castles to mark their victories, and around the castles they set up special towns called boroughs for their Norman followers. Monks from France came to open priories in these Norman boroughs, and William and his barons took control of the English Church. It seemed that the way of life of the Anglo-Saxon people was about to be changed completely by these new invaders. Perhaps the Welsh people were glad to see their Anglo-Saxon enemies being defeated by the Normans.

But before long, the Normans had reached the borders of Wales. Although the land was not as fertile as in England, William wanted to conquer it so that he would become the King of Britain as well as the Duke of Normandy. However, he had too many problems in England and Normandy to bother with Wales himself. Instead, William decided to ask three of his most powerful barons to look after Wales. These three barons were given lands near the Welsh border. He gave William Fitzosbern land in Hereford in the south. In the centre he made Roger Montgomery Earl of Shrewsbury. In the north the trusty Hugh of Avranches, or Hugh the Fat as he was sometimes called, was given lands around Chester. Soon these three barons began to attack the neighbouring Welsh kingdoms. The lands they conquered were then given to the barons' favourite knights.

Statue of William the Conqueror on horseback, and his tomb in Caen Cathedral, France

Within thirty years, by 1093, these strong Norman lords had won their way into Gwynedd in the north, into Gwent, Glamorgan and the Gower in the south, and as far as Cardigan and down into Pembroke in the centre. The Welsh people didn't know what had happened. The Welsh chroniclers speak of the 'injustice, oppression and violence of these French invaders'. One churchman, called Rhygyfarch, wrote in a Latin poem that:

'People and priests are mocked by everything the French do. They add to our oppression and eat our foods. We shall be made prisoners and slaves, we shall be without comfort'. It seemed as though the Norman French had conquered Wales too and that the Welsh way of life could be destroyed for ever.

And yet, we know today that the Normans had not really conquered the whole of Wales by 1093. It took them almost another two hundred years to capture Gwynedd completely. Almost five hundred years would pass before Wales and England were united in an Act of Union.

This book will try to explain why the Normans and the English took so long to conquer Wales, and to describe the events which took place during these five hundred years in the history of Wales.

Two scenes from the Bayeux Tapestry: Normans advancing on horseback (*left*), Saxon footsoldiers (*right*)

Building a Motte and Bailey Castle

When we talk of a 'castle' today , we usually mean a huge stone building built many hundreds of years ago. But the first castles in Wales were not made of stone at all. They were built by the Norman invaders and they were made of wood. The wood has now rotted away, and the buildings have disappeared completely.

How can we find out where these early castles used to be? The easiest way is to travel over Wales in an aeroplane. The Normans built their wooden castles on large mounds of earth. Looking down from an aeroplane it is easy to pick out these mounds. If you fly all over Wales you can spot where hundreds of these early Norman castles used to be, especially in the border area between England and Wales. This was the area the Norman barons settled first, and was called the Marches of Wales.

One of the first timber castles to be built in Wales was at Montgomery, on the river Severn in mid-Wales. It was called Montgomery by its owner, Roger, who came from the town of St Foi de Montgommeri in France. He was made the Earl of Shrewsbury by William the Conqueror. Let's think back to Montgomery in the year 1084, to learn how this timber castle was built and what shape it was.

The site of the castle is a hive of activity. Some men are digging up earth and filling baskets with it, and others are carrying the baskets up a slope and dumping the earth on top of a mound. One man looks as if he's in charge of the workers. Let's see if we can find out more from him about the work of building an early Norman castle.

'The easiest way for me to explain', he says in Norman French, 'is by drawing a plan of the finished castle'. He draws in the mud with his finger. 'Now', he continues, 'you can see the workers digging a ditch and using the earth they are removing to build this huge mound. When the mound is high enough we'll build a wooden tower on top of it'. He draws the outline of a square wooden tower.

'*Who will live there?*', we ask.

'The owner, or lord and his family, of

Motte (mound)

Bailey

Moat

Reconstruction of a motte and bailey castle

course. You see, a Norman castle is a home as well as a safe and protected place. Around the tower we're going to build a high wooden fence with a platform on it, so that the soldiers can keep watch over the countryside around. This part of a Norman castle is called the motte.'

'What about this flat, oval piece of land outside the motte?'

'That is called the bailey', he explains, as he marks a number of small buildings on his drawing. 'When we're ready we'll build a kitchen, a barn, a chapel, rooms for the soldiers, and a smithy in the bailey. These will be protected by a strong fence and a ditch.'

'But how will you get from the motte to the bailey? Will you have to go down into the ditch every time?'

'No, of course not. In fact in many of our motte and bailey castles back in France, the ditch is filled with water, so that's impossible. No, we'll build a wooden bridge. If ever the castle is attacked by enemies, we'll be able to run up to the motte and draw up part of the bridge to stop them coming in.'

'You seem to have plenty of work ahead of you', we say. *'It's lucky you've got such good workers to help you'.*

'Mmm ... I wouldn't say "to help us". They're local Welsh people. We've conquered their lands and now they *have* to work for us. Mind you, this is a rush job because we need this castle quickly. It will only take a week or two to finish the motte and bailey. People will be able to see the castle from miles away. That will make the Welsh people realise that the new lords who have settled in the Marches of Wales are very, very powerful. We'll also be able to go out to attack the other parts of mid-Wales from our castle here at Montgomery, and it won't take us long to conquer it.'

This Norman's words proved to be very true. The lords of the Marches did use their rough-and-ready motte and bailey castles to help them to conquer many lands and kingdoms in Wales. But although the castles must

This scene from the Bayeux Tapestry shows men piling up a motte

have looked frightening, they did have weak points. The wooden fences and towers could be set on fire and destroyed easily in a raid. Because of this the Normans soon replaced the wooden castles with stone ones. The stone towers, or keeps, were often too heavy for the man-made earth mounds, so the Normans had to find new places to build them. At Montgomery the new stone castle was built a mile away from the old motte and bailey castle of timber and earth, many years later. Today the site of the first castle is called *'Yr Hen Domen'*, the old earth mound.

Aerial view of the remains of a motte and bailey castle

Welsh Against Normans in Gwynedd

We can follow the story of how the Normans tried to conquer North Wales in several books and manuscripts written at the time. But there are two special accounts of the Norman campaign, which look at the events from very different viewpoints.

One was written by a monk called Orderic Vitalis who lived in Norman times. He came from Shrewsbury on the Welsh border, but was sent to live in a monastery in Normandy. Orderic admired the Normans and his book describes their successes with great pride.

Another book tells the life-story of Gruffudd ap Cynan, one of the royal princes of Gwynedd, who fought for twenty-five years to win back his kingdom. It seems that Gruffudd's son, Owain Gwynedd paid for this life-story to be written, so we can be sure that the writer will only mention Gruffudd's good deeds. The author praises Gruffudd and his Welsh followers, of course, and usually describes the Normans as the enemy. Although these two books are so different, if we use them together we can build up a good picture of what happened in North Wales during the first years of the Norman conquest.

As we have seen, when William of Normandy had conquered England, he asked his faithful baron Earl Hugh of Chester to look after North Wales for him. At once, Earl Hugh and his knights began to attack the Welsh kingdoms. Soon they arrived at Rhuddlan. Here they built a castle and set up a town for their followers. The earl put his nephew Robert in charge of the castle, and told him to carry on trying to take over North Wales. As Orderic says, Robert of Rhuddlan was very ambitious and ruthless. His aim was to destroy the Welsh princes and to become the Lord of

The ruins of Degannwy Castle, Gwynedd

Gwynedd. On and on he went, until he arrived at Degannwy where he built a castle to celebrate his victory. Even Orderic found it difficult to stomach Robert's cruel ways. He says that 'for fifteen years Robert plundered the Welsh without mercy . . . he slaughtered some on the spot like cattle, others he kept in chains for years'.

One of the most important Welsh princes who tried to oppose Robert of Rhuddlan was Gruffudd ap Cynan. His life-story tells us how he was brought up in Ireland and how he became determined to return to Gwynedd to claim his father's kingdom. At first he worked with Robert against another prince of Gwynedd, and then he turned and attacked the castle at Rhuddlan. After several years of fighting between the Welsh princes themselves, and also between the Welsh princes and the Normans, Robert managed to trick Gruffudd and to imprison him in Chester gaol. Robert also decided to punish the Welsh for supporting Gruffudd. He cut off the right thumb of every soldier's hand so that none of them would ever be able to use bows and arrows again.

Poor Gruffudd remained in prison for many years, until he was rescued by fellow Welshmen. Then he began to attack Robert and the Normans again. In 1088 he brought three ships ashore near Degannwy Castle. Orderic will tell the bloodthirsty tale himself.

'The Welsh king Gruffudd landed with three ships (near) the Great Orme. Gruffudd and his men swooped on the lands and carried off men and beasts ... Meanwhile the cries of the crowd raised Robert from a mid-day sleep ... The anger of the Lord Marcher, a man as brave as a lion, knew no bounds, and he ordered the few men with him to fall on the Welsh ... They protested that they were too few in number and that the way down from the top of the rock was too steep. Then Robert, accompanied by only one knight, rushed on the enemy. When they saw him with only a shield for protection ... they flung their javelins at this valiant lord, bore down his shield ... and fatally wounded him. At last the nobel warrior, riddled with darts, fell to his knees (and died). Then they all rushed up to him, cut off his head and fixed it on the mast of a ship as a sign of victory.'

But even with the hated Robert of Rhuddlan dead, the Welsh could not forget the Normans. Earl Hugh of Chester now continued with Robert's work, and he and Gruffudd were at war for several years. Gradually Gruffudd became stronger and stronger, and Henry I, on becoming King of England, seems to have decided to allow Gruffudd to rule the Kingdom of Gwynedd peacefully.

The life-story describes these last thirty-seven years of Gruffudd ap Cynan's reign, and shows how successful he was. It says that:

'The people began to build churches in every acre, and to sow and plant some trees, and to make orchards and gardens and surround them with meadows and ditches and to rebuild ruins.'

After many years of fighting and bitter conflict, Gruffudd ap Cynan had succeeded in preparing the way for the future great princes of Gwynedd. His kingdom had survived the first wave of great Norman attacks after all.

The Marriage of Princess Nest of Deheubarth

The ruins of Cilgerran Castle, Dyfed

Even during the first years of the Norman conquest, the Welsh and the Normans were not always at one another's throats. Some tried to live at peace with one another. One way of achieving this was through marriage, as the story of Nest, Princess of Deheubarth, shows.

Sometime around 1100, Nest married Gerald of Windsor, the Norman constable of Pembroke Castle. We do not know whether she was forced into the marriage or whether she was allowed to choose her own husband, but for the daughter of the important royal house of Deheubarth it was a strange move. Her father, the great King Rhys ap Tewdwr, had been killed by the Normans who had then swept through his kingdom and taken his family's lands.

Gerald of Windsor was a Norman who was feared and respected by the Welsh people. They could still remember how, four years earlier, he and his soldiers had survived a great Welsh attack on Pembroke Castle. For months the Welsh army surrounded the castle and waited for Gerald and his men to be starved out and to surrender. But Gerald played a clever trick on the Welsh. He pretended that he had plenty of food left inside the castle gates and that the siege could go on for many more months. In fact, he had only four pigs and a little grain left, to feed his starving soldiers. But instead of feeding his own men, he cooked hams and threw them over the castle walls into the arms of the Welsh soldiers – telling them to share in his feast of plenty.

The Welsh soldiers couldn't understand it at all. How could there be enough food inside the castle? Was Gerald some kind of magician? The Welsh lost heart and decided that there was no point trying to conquer Pembroke Castle. Gerald won his fight against the Welsh through his cunning.

Gerald also won an important prize when he married Princess Nest. As her husband he could claim a right to the lands of the Kingdom of Deheubarth. As Gerald's famous grandson Gerald the Welshman says, he married Nest so that 'he might sink his roots and those of his family more deeply in those parts'. Nest was also, it seems, a very beautiful woman. This beauty brought her and her family into great trouble on one occasion, according to a story written in the *Brut* or *Chronicle of the Princes*. The events took place at Christmas-time in the year 1109. Gerald and his family were celebrating the holiday at Cilgerran Castle in Dyfed. Nearby, at Cardigan Castle, one of the main lords of Powys was holding a great feast, and he invited his son Owain to join him in the hall. After eating and drinking, the young men began to discuss the beauty of Princess Nest. At once, Owain decided to go to find Nest so that he could judge her beauty for himself. He set out to visit her at Cilgerran.

As soon as Owain saw Nest he fell in love with her, and swore that he would have the Welsh princess for himself. Within a few nights he and about fourteen companions returned to capture her. They dug their way in, raised the alarm and began to set the castle on fire. The *Brut* continues with the story:

'And Gerald woke up and was frightened when he saw what time it was. And his wife told him "Don't go to the door because your enemies are around. Come with me," and she led him to the little room by the side of the house and Gerald escaped through the hole in the small room'.

It seems that the great Norman knight, Gerald of Windsor, was forced to escape from the Welsh prince Owain through the shute used as a toilet! Can you imagine how the brave and cunning Gerald must have felt?

Once Gerald had escaped, Owain rushed into the room, seized Nest and her children, and carried them off to Cardigan Castle. Later Nest seems to have persuaded the dashing Owain to set her and the children free. But through his reckless daring Owain stirred up the anger of the King of England himself, and Owain and his family were made to pay for his deeds for many years.

Eventually Owain joined King Henry of England's side, and began to help Henry fight against the Welshmen of Dyfed. During one battle Owain found himself fighting on the same side as his old enemy, Gerald of Windsor. As they were leaving the battlefield, Gerald and his men attacked Owain and his soldiers. In the fight that followed Gerald killed Owain, and so paid him back for the way he had insulted an important Norman lord and his Welsh princess.

A gold finger ring from Llantrithyd, set with garnet, which dates from the time of Princess Nest

Princess Gwenllian's Brave Stand

The year is 1136. King Henry I of England has just died, and the Welsh princes of South Wales have risen in revolt against the Norman conquerors. At his court in Ystrad Tywi, Deheubarth, Gruffudd ap Rhys ap Tewdwr (Princess Nest's brother) is discussing his next move with his wife Gwenllian.

Gwenllian, I haven't got enough soldiers or weapons to win in battle against the strong Norman Lords. I shall have to seek help from the Kingdom of Gwynedd.

Yes, you must go at once, Lord Gruffudd. My father, Gruffudd ap Cynan, and my two brothers will help you. Hurry! There is no time to waste.

Take care while I'm gone, Gwenllian. Look after my sons.

I shall, don't worry. Return safely, my Lord.

BUT WHILE GRUFFUDD IS AWAY A MESSENGER BRINGS BAD NEWS TO GWENLLIAN'S COURT

Lady Gwenllian, the Norman lord Maurice de Londres — from Cydweli Castle — is gathering together a huge army to attack the Welsh.

What can we do? My Lord Gruffudd is away in North Wales.

I have no choice. I must lead my people against the Norman oppressors.

But my lady, that is impossible. You are a woman and a princess. We cannot have a woman leading an army into battle.

Woman or princess, I must lead the army. I cannot allow the Normans to take our lands without fighting for them. Come, we must gather our men at once.

Mother, may I come with you? I am old enough to fight for my country now.

And I want to come too, Mother.

O no! I would prefer you to stay at home, Morgan and Maelgwn. But if you feel you must come, then I shall be proud of you. I hope Maredudd and Rhys will be safe here at Ystrad Tywi.

MEANWHILE THE NORMAN KNIGHT, MAURICE DE LONDRES, SETS OUT WITH HIS ARMY FROM CYDWELI CASTLE TO FIGHT AND CONQUER THE WELSH

AS GWENLLIAN RIDES TOWARDS CYDWELI, MORE AND MORE WELSHMEN JOIN HER BAND OF WARRIORS. SOME FARM WORKERS PICK UP THE NEAREST FARM TOOLS AND FOLLOW THE WELSH PRINCESS.

ON A HILL NEAR CYDWELI CASTLE THE TWO ARMIES COME FACE TO FACE. THEY FIGHT A HARD, CRUEL BATTLE. SLOWLY THE WELSH ARE DEFEATED.

BRAVE GWENLLIAN AND HER SON MORGAN ARE KILLED, AND THE WELSH LOSE HEART.

MAELGWN IS CAPTURED AND TAKEN PRISONER BY THE NORMANS

And so, Gwenllian's stand against the Norman lords of south-west Wales ended in disaster. Gruffudd ap Rhys and his friends from Gwynedd arrived too late to save the Welsh army. Within a year Gruffudd himself was dead and his small kingdom lay in the hands of his two youngest sons, Maredudd and Rhys. Yet Gwenllian's sacrifice is remembered in Wales today, and the land on which the battle was fought is still known as Maes Gwenllian.

Farming in the Welshry

This longhouse, Hendre'r Ywydd Uchaf, has been reconstructed to show what it originally looked like outside and inside

On a farm in the Welshry in Wales it is springtime, and the farmer is ready to plough the land and sow his seeds. The way Welsh farmers help one another with the ploughing is different from the open field and manorial system of the Normans.

The Welsh farmers work together in teams of twelve. Each member of the team has an important part to play. Eight of the twelve each provides an ox to pull the heavy plough. The ninth person is a blacksmith who makes and owns the iron parts of the plough, while the tenth is a carpenter who makes and owns its wooden parts. The last two members of the team are a ploughman and a caller. The caller's job is to call and shout at the oxen to make them work harder. The ploughman has to plough his own land first. The other members of the team examine his work carefully, then tell him that their lands must be ploughed in the same way, and up to the same standard.

Cattle are very important on this Welsh farm. Cows provide milk, butter, cheese, meat and leather. Oxen are useful for pulling heavy loads and, of course, for ploughing. Most farmers in the Welshry have about two oxen, three cows, a horse and perhaps six sheep. Sheep didn't become popular in Wales until

monks, who were brought over by the Normans, began to keep huge flocks.

When the ploughing is over, and as summer approaches, it is time for the farmer to move his animals to graze the higher mountain land. The whole family prepares to carry its belongings to its summer house or *hafod* (*haf* means summer). One farmer in Ardudwy, Gwynedd, was fined in 1336 for not moving some of his animals up into the *hafod* for the summer.

The winter house is called a *hendre* (which means old town) and these names, *hafod* and *hendre*, can often be found on farms and homes in Wales today. Can you think of any examples?

As the *hafod* will only be used for the summer months, the farmer does not make a great effort to build a strong house. He works in a hurry and uses whatever materials he can find nearby. Nowadays most of these temporary, miserable hovels have disappeared, but we can guess how they would have been built.

The farmer prepares wooden poles and places them to stand in the shape of a small hut. Between the poles he puts a layer of brushwood, then he gathers sods of turf to put in layers against the brushwood. The grassy side of the turf faces the inside of the hut. Can you imagine living in a house with grass on its walls?

What can the farmer use to roof his simple house? He can thatch it with reeds, or he can use turf again. He doesn't build a chimney to carry away the smoke, but leaves a small hole in the roof. Unfortunately this doesn't work very well, and the hut is often filled with smoke from the peat fire.

The tiny hole left for a window has no glass in it. Dirty old rags keep out the worst of the wind and rain. Inside the *hafod* the floor is bare earth and it is dark, damp and gloomy. Even though these *hafotai* are only in use for the six months of summer, they must be miserable places to live in.

As autumn approaches, the farmer moves his family and animals back to their winter home in the *hendre*. Although better than the *hafod*, the *hendre* is not a dream home, either. It is built of wattle, or woven twigs and daub, a mixture of clay, mud and cowhair. It may be roofed with thatch, turf or sometimes local slates covered with whitewash.

The *hendre* was often a longhouse, with the farmer and his family living at one end, and the animals at the other. Sometimes a passageway or partition was put up to separate the two ends. Can this be the kind of house so vividly described in the old Welsh legend 'The Dream of Rhonabwy'?

'They saw an old hall, very black and high, with a great deal of smoke pouring out of it. When they entered they found the floor uneven and full of puddles, and where it sloped it was difficult to stand on it, it was so slippery with the mud and dung of cattle. Where there were puddles a man could go up to his ankles in water and dirt ... And when they came to the hall ... they saw that it was very gloomy ... On one side of the fire was a yellow calfskin on the floor and it was a great privilege to anyone who could get on to that skin.'

Once again, because they were built of such poor materials, very few Welsh longhouses have survived. A visit to Hendre'r Ywydd Uchaf farmhouse at the Welsh Folk Museum near Cardiff can give us some idea of how a Welsh longhouse looked. If we use our imaginations and add the heavy smell of smoke from a peat fire, the stench of cow dung, the buzz of flies, and fleas biting everywhere, our picture of a Welsh farmer's longhouse in the Welshry during the Middle Ages will be even clearer.

The remains of a wooden disc wheel from Dolanog which dates from the 12th century

Farming on a Norman Manor

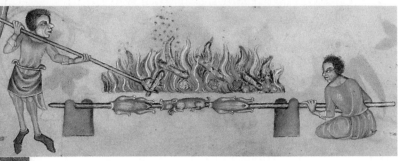

Food being spit-roasted on an open fire

Look at this picture of a special kind of farming found on the Gower peninsula in West Glamorgan. You can see that the large fields are divided into long, equal strips. The strips are worked by different farmers, yet there are no hedges or fences between them to mark off one person's land from another's. There is only a grassy bank to separate them. This kind of farming has been going on here for about nine hundred years, since Norman times.

The Norman conquerors were hungry for land. As soon as they had defeated the Welsh princes in battle and built their motte and bailey castles to defend their new lands, they began to settle down as farmers. Often the Norman lords would take over the old Welsh system of farming, but on the more fertile lands, especially on Gower, in the Vale of Glamorgan, and on the border between England and Wales, they introduced their own way of farming.

A piece of land belonging to a Norman lord or knight was called a manor. The owner lived in a manor house or castle. He kept about one third of the land for himself and rented the rest out to tenants – freemen and villeins.

Let's imagine we're back in the twelfth century, and can take a closer look at this type of farming on Gower. We can see a peasant busy ploughing in a field. He seems rather reluctant to stop and talk to us at first.

'I can't really spare the time to talk', he says. 'I must finish ploughing this strip of land for my lord today, or he won't be too pleased. I have to work on his land for three days every week and at busy times, during the harvest, I sometimes work five or six days a week for him.'

'*Does he pay you well?*' we ask politely. The ploughman looks at us in surprise.

'Pay me well? On no! In fact I have to do a great deal of work for nothing. You see, I live in one of his cottages at Rhosili village, nearby, and he lets me farm eighteen acres for myself. I pay for these by working for him on certain days. I have to find building wood and firewood for him, too.'

'*Have you always lived and worked here at Rhosili?*'

'Indeed not. Look over there, across the sea', he says, pointing out over the blue water. 'That's where I come from, Somerset. I get very homesick sometimes when it's a clear day and I can see my dear old country'.

'*Why don't you go back, if you're not happy here on Gower?*'

'I can't, I can't. You see I'm not a freeman. I'm a villein. I can't leave this manor without my lord's permission. My Norman lord conquered my old Saxon master back in Somerset, and he forced me to move with him to farm his new land here on Gower. The Normans have no mercy. They've grabbed all the best farming lands for themselves and driven the Welsh who used to live here out into the Welshry, up in the hills and mountains.'

'*Tell us a little more about this strip farming*', we prompt. '*Is it a good way to farm?*'

'Mmm – there are good and bad points about it. You see my strips of land aren't all together in one patch. I'll have one strip here and one way over on the other side of the field, perhaps, so that everyone has a fair share of the best and the worst land. These strips are changed every year by the manor court. The court also tells me which crops to grow and where. This year I have to grow wheat on some of my strips and the others I shall leave empty.'

'*Isn't that a waste?*'

'Not really, even good land like this can't grow wheat year after year without a rest. I do find it a waste of time to have to walk from one strip to the other, though'

Milking a cow

'*And what about cattle? It must be hard work stopping them from wandering on to your neighbour's patch.*'

'It is! But they usually graze in the hedged-in meadows around the open fields, or out on the waste or common lands near the village. But you must excuse me now. The lord's bailiff will be here soon to inspect my work, and I must finish my ploughing.'

And so the new Norman conquerors, their freemen, villeins and serfs settled to farm the best lands in Wales. Others settled as craftsmen and tradesmen in the small towns or boroughs that grew up around the Norman castles, at Cardiff, Newport and Brecon. The town of Rhuddlan was described in King William's famous 'Domesday Book' of 1086 as having its own church, mills, fisheries, a mint for making money and a furnace for making iron. It also had eighteen burgesses or towns-people. The Normans had come to stay.

220 yards
(201 metres)

When a farmer ploughed a strip field the earth was always thrown to the right by the plough. The centre of the strip built up to form a 'ridge' while the outside formed a 'furrow'. This helped to keep the land well drained

22 feet
(6.7 metres)

Cosmeston – a Norman Medieval Village

(*above*) Artist's reconstruction of the kilnhouse and (*inset*) rethatching in progress

Let's go on a visit to find out more about how the Normans settled in Wales. This time we shall travel down to the Vale of Glamorgan, a fertile area of Wales where the Normans established many manors. One of these was at Cosmeston near Penarth.

A team of local archaeologists is busy clearing and excavating the site of the manor. They hope to rebuild the medieval village of Cosmeston. The work is very slow, as they have to be careful not to destroy valuable evidence of the past. One of the archaeologists kindly agrees to explain the work they are doing.

'This would have been a typical Norman manor, with a manor house at its centre and open fields around the village. But we've decided to start our work down in the village with the peasant buildings. We've taken care to rebuild everything exactly where it used to stand and to make sure we know how it was used. Come with me and I'll show you what I mean.'

He leads us towards a tiny stone building with a thatched roof. What can it have been used for?

'This was the kilnhouse for the manor', he explains. 'As you can see it has been built of limestone. This was collected from Lavernock beach nearby. The stones have been shaped and worked so that they lie neatly on top of one another in courses. Between the joints, to hold the stones together, we've used a mixture of local clay, dung and soil, as people would have done in medieval times. If you look up at the roof, you will see that it is thatched with reeds from the wetlands nearby. Come inside and we can see the roof properly.'

It is dark but quite cosy inside. In fact there seems to be a lingering smell of freshly-baked bread. Can we be imagining it?

'Let me show you how the roof was made', continues our guide. 'Can you see the withies – the willow and hazel rods – woven between the willow rafters? They help to hold the thatch in place. Now look carefully at the inside of the kilnhouse. At one end is the kiln for drying the grains from the harvest, and at the other end you can see a bread-baking oven. We're quite proud of this oven because it works very well. On special days we hold medieval events here at Cosmeston, and we can bake 120 loaves a day to sell to the tourists who visit the village.'

We move on from the kilnhouse to a pair of stone and thatch buildings. These look like peasants' homes, and the archaeologist says that we've guessed correctly. There is only one room in each house. The whole family must have cooked, eaten and slept all in the same room. Yet these stone buildings were not as poor and miserable as most of the homes of the Welsh peasants in medieval times.

Next, the guide leads us to the site of a medieval farm.

'This is one of the most interesting groups of buildings at Cosmeston', he says enthusiastically. 'Some Welsh farms were longhouses where the farmer, his family and the animals all lived under the same roof. Here we can see that there used to be three buildings around a central yard. One would have been the farmhouse, one the barn and in the middle would have been the byre or animal house. We keep animals such as sheep, goats and ducks here to help to bring the farm to life once more.'

As he leads us from the farmstead, we notice a group of men clearing and digging a patch of land. They are dressed like medieval peasants, and the implements they use are crude and old-fashioned. Our guide tells us that they are trying to re-create a peasant's garden, growing vegetables such as leeks, onions, garlic, peas and beans and all kinds of herbs which will be used for cooking and for making medicines.

Obviously the work of re-creating a medieval village at Cosmeston is going to take time and patience, but it is an exciting project which can help us to understand how ordinary people lived on the Norman manors of Wales. Unfortunately, we shall never know the names of the people who lived in these medieval houses or find out exactly what

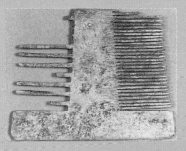

A medieval bone comb found at Cosmeston

happened to them. Why did these stone houses fall into ruin? Why did the medieval village at Cosmeston disappear? Our guide is willing to suggest one possible answer.

'It seems that during the first years after the Normans arrived, the population of England and Wales grew and grew. Then the weather became colder and wetter and before long it became difficult to grow enough food for all these people, and a famine developed. The people became weak and when the disease called the Black Death swept through the country in the middle of the fourteenth century, many people died and many villages had to be abandoned.'

This could explain what happened at Cosmeston. Now, 650 years later, this medieval village is being brought to life again.

The Normans and the Church in Wales

One of the main buildings in every village and town in Wales is the parish church. The stone towers often rise up above the houses and shops. Most of these churches were built during the twelfth and thirteenth centuries, when the Normans were slowly conquering Wales.

Look at these pictures of the parish church of Llanbadarn, near Aberystwyth, Dyfed. Can you see the lovely Norman archway and the square bell-tower? Does it remind you of a castle tower? The Normans realised how important the Church was in Wales.

But not everything about the Welsh Church was bad. There were still many holy men and scholars in Wales. At Llanbadarn church, for example, Sulien and his sons and grandsons were famous scholars and teachers. One son, Ieuan, was a poet who decorated manuscripts with beautiful designs. Another son, Rhygyfarch, wrote the well-known life-story of St David. He wanted to show that Welsh saints were just as powerful as Norman saints.

The Normans, however, were determined

Llanbadarn Fawr Church

The early Norman entrance arch

The Welsh Church had changed a great deal since the age of St David and the other saints, five hundred years before. The early saints settled and built their churches in poor, isolated places. Now churches were wealthy, and the abbots or bishops behaved like rich gentlemen. Many of them were married, and jobs were passed down from father to son. The Welsh Church still looked towards Ireland for leadership rather than towards Rome and the Pope as the Norman Church did.

to take over the Welsh Church so that they could rule the Welsh more effectively. They were also greedy for the land and riches of the Church. Their first step was to place Normans as bishops in the cathedral churches instead of the Welsh bishops. Earl Hugh of Chester was the first to do this. He made Hervé from Brittany Bishop of Bangor in Gwynedd in 1092. But Hervé didn't last long. As you can imagine, the Welsh people didn't like him. He had to have an army of knights to protect him every time he went out. His life was threatened and members of his family were murdered. Hervé had to leave Bangor in disgrace.

The Welsh may have got rid of Hervé, but the Normans were still too powerful for them. The Welsh cathedrals in St Davids, Llandaff and St Asaph soon had Norman bishops and the Welsh people were then forced to accept the Archbishop of Canterbury as the most important leader of the Church in England and Wales.

The new Norman bishops did try to win over the support of the Welsh people. One of them, Bishop Urban of Llandaff, tried to prove that his cathedral church had a long and magnificent Welsh history. He tried to make St Dyfrig, the main Welsh saint of south-east Wales in the sixth century, important again. He did this by building a special tomb in the cathedral church. Then he sent some of his priests on the treacherous journey to Bardsey Island in Gwynedd. According to Welsh legend, there are 20,000 saints buried on this holy island. The priests were expected to find St Dyfrig's bones, and bring them back safely to be placed in the tomb in Llandaff cathedral. It must have been a very difficult task to know which were St Dyfrig's bones after so many centuries. The priests returned with the casket and Bishop Urban felt proud that such an important Welshman was now buried at Llandaff.

A monk inscribing a manuscript in the twelfth century

A page from Rhygyfarch's Psalter probably decorated by his brother Ieuan

Bardsey Island

Another step the Normans took to control the Welsh Church was to divide the country up into parishes. Some parishes were very small, others were quite big. At the centre of each parish stood the parish church, rebuilt in stone. Many of the churches were painted with whitewash in the beginning, and those of Gwynedd were said to shine like stars in heaven. These parish churches can still be seen in Wales today, and each one has an interesting story of its own to tell.

The White Monks in Wales

Part of a thirteenth-century tile from Whitland Abbey, showing the Lamb of God

Can you imagine what it must be like to leave your family and friends forever, to go to live with a group of strangers in a monastery for the rest of your life? Monks or nuns who lived in monasteries or abbeys had to give up everything they owned. They were not allowed to marry and they had to obey many strict rules. It sounds a hard way of life.

Yet many people were attracted to this kind of life in the twelfth and thirteenth centuries in Wales. Some of them dressed in long black robes and said they followed the teaching of St Benedict. They were called Benedictine monks. The Norman lords, who came to conquer Wales, supported these 'black' monks. Their monasteries were built in the shadows of the great Norman castles in towns such as Brecon, Monmouth and Pembroke.

The Welsh people were rather suspicious of these 'black' Benedictines. Many of the monks were foreigners from Normandy. It isn't surprising to learn that some of them were advised to 'strengthen the locks of your doors, and surround your monastery with a good ditch and a very strong wall', in order to keep out the Welsh people.

The Welsh princes and people did take another kind of monk to their hearts. These were the Cistercians, and they were brought from Citeaux in France to Wales by the Norman lords. They were called 'white' monks because their long robes of wool were not dyed. Monasteries like Tintern in Gwent, Margam and Neath were very Norman at the beginning but became more Welsh.

Then a group of white monks came to settle at Whitland, Dyfed. They became popular and soon the Welsh princes began to give them gifts of land and to help Whitland open other houses throughout Wales. Let's visit one of these new Cistercian abbeys to learn about the monks' way of life. The year is 1201 and the abbey of Valle Crucis (Latin for Valley of the Cross) in Clwyd is just being built. As we approach, we see and hear the masons and carpenters busy on the new building.

The abbot Philip, who is head of the monastery, is interviewing a young Welsh lad called Thomas, who wants to become a monk. Abbot Philip is trying to show him that life in an abbey is not an easy, comfortable one. 'You do realise, young Thomas, that Cistercian monks spend a third of their time praying and worshipping God?', he asks.

'Yes, I do', answers Thomas, 'I was told that you have seven services a day and that the first one is at three o'clock in the morning!'.

'That's right, then another third of your time will be spent working. You may be copying manuscripts in the monastery itself or working out in the fields. We shall have to work hard here at Valle Crucis. You may find yourself driving a plough, helping with the harvest or looking after the sheep', says the abbot.

'I'm quite used to that, Abbot Philip', is the answer, 'I was brought up on a farm about six miles from here'.

'But what about the food? Monks aren't allowed to eat meat at all. You will get two meals, a pound of bread and a pint of wine a day.' Thomas looks a little worried. 'And you'll have to learn not to speak at all during mealtimes in the refectory. If you disobey these rules you can be whipped with a stick on your bare back.'

Thomas is silent for a minute. Then he asks, 'But what if I want someone to pass me a drink or the salt?'

'You will have to learn the signals monks use', replies Philip. 'Look, what do you think this is?' He shakes his hand on its side and then holds it still. Thomas has no idea. 'That's the sign for a fish', says Abbot Philip. 'You'll soon learn. Would you be able to read to the other monks in Latin during the mealtimes in the refectory?'

'I can't read at all, abbot', says Thomas sadly.

'Don't worry,' answers Philip, 'you can learn to read and write here. But are you sure you wish to join us to become a novice monk in Valle Crucis monastery?'

'Yes I am', replies Thomas. 'I wish to serve God by being a white monk.'

There must have been many young men like Thomas in Wales at this time because there were about sixty monks living in every Cistercian abbey. We know the names of a hundred of these monks because they signed

The main features of Valle Crucis Abbey

1 The main entrance
2 Nave – lay brothers came to services here
3 Choir crossing – the monks' seven main services of the day were held here
4 Transepts – the monks' night stair from their dormitory was found in the south transept
5 The site of the high altar
6 Fishpond
7 Cloister
8 East range – this contained the monks' dormitory and day rooms
9 Chapter House – the monks met here each day to listen to a chapter of their *Rule*
10 Monks' toilet
11 Monks' refectory
12 Kitchen
13 West range – this contained a dining room and dormitory for the lay brothers

their names on documents and papers.

But what about Valle Crucis abbey? Let's ask the abbot to tell us more about it.

'This is a very exciting project', he begins, 'I used to be a monk at Strata Marcella abbey in Powys, but is was so full that I was invited to take a group of monks to start a new monastery here in Valle Crucis. So we will be

the daughter house of Strata Marcella, which is itself the daughter house of the famous Whitland Abbey in Dyfed.'

'*Wasn't there some trouble at Strata Marcella some years ago?*' we ask, rather shyly.

'I hoped you wouldn't mention that', answers Philip. 'Yes, there was. Monks, as you know, aren't supposed to have anything to do with women. Well, poor abbot Enoch fell in love with a nun and ran away with her! But he soon realised his mistake. He returned to the monastery and admitted before God that he had broken the rules.'

'*Tell us, abbot*', we ask, '*how did you find this lovely spot, on the banks of the river Eglwyseg and just below the fort of Dinas Bran, for your monastery?*'

'We were very fortunate. We were given the land by the Welsh prince of North Powys, Madog ap Gruffudd. He wanted to please God by giving land to the Church and he felt that the white monks would be more popular than the black monks in Powys. Look, I can show you the charter he gave us which says quite clearly which land is ours. But you must excuse me now. I have more interviews to hold – we need a cook, a chamberlain, more lay brothers … '

Abbot Philip walks away in a hurry and we take another look at Valle Crucis's charter. Little did the abbot realise that abbey charters such as this one would be kept safely for centuries, and are now in museums and archive offices in Wales, even though the monasteries themselves were closed down long ago. Another roll of paper lies next to the charter. It is a plan of the monastery showing where the new buildings will be. Work has already begun on the most important building, the church, and we can see that the windows are going to be high and beautiful. The cloister next to the church will be used for reading and thinking. Around the cloister will be the chapter house, where the monks will hear one chapter of the rule of the monastery read every day, the refectory, the kitchen and a rere-dorter or toilet.

On the plan we can see the transcept where the night stairs from the monks' dormitory (above the chapter house) lead down into the church. Thanks to the stairs, the monks will be able to hurry down quickly to the church for the early service at three o'clock in the morning. In fact Abbot Philip's plan for Valle Crucis has not been kept safely for us to look at today, but we can work out how the buildings would have appeared at this time by studying the ruined walls and from the work of archaeologists. This work has shown that a hall was built especially for the abbot, as leader of the monastery, some 250 years after abbot Philip's time.

Valle Crucis Abbey today

Poets have also described the beauty of Valle Crucis monastery. Tudur Aled, the poet, called it 'the splendid home of the high country'. Another Welsh poet, Guto'r Glyn, spent his last years, when he was old and blind, as a guest at the monastery. To him, as to so many Welsh people, living in an age of constant fighting and cruel disease, the peace of the Cistercian abbeys was like heaven on earth.

Hangers on at a Monastery

Most monasteries in the Middle Ages were surrounded by a stone wall. The monks had, after all, chosen to cut themselves off from the world. Travellers were expected to stop at the gatehouse, and special monks would be chosen to look after them.

The almoner looked after the poor and the beggars. He was to be kind and merciful towards them, to give clothes to those who were naked, and food and drink to the hungry and thirsty. According to one writer, Gerald de Barry, the monastery at Margam was famous for its help to the poor. Gerald proves his point by telling a story.

Towards the end of the twelfth century there was a terrible famine. Large crowds flocked to Margam to beg food at the gatehouse. The almoner had none to give, so he sent a ship to Bristol to fetch grain. But the wind turned and the sailing ship could not return. Everyone was in despair. Then a miracle happened. The monks found that a field of wheat near the abbey had ripened overnight, a month before its time. They harvested it and fed the starving people. From this story would you say that Gerald liked and supported the white monks of Margam?

Prisoner taking sanctuary with monks

Another building which was part of the monastery was the hospital. Old and sick monks and local people came here for help. When they were ill, monks were allowed to eat meat. At a time when there were no other hospitals or homes for old people, the kindness and loving care of the monks were very important in the Welsh countryside.

Ordinary travellers also looked for shelter in the monasteries. Many of these were pilgrims travelling to other churches and abbeys to worship. The guests were looked after and were given nourishing meals and clean beds. Unfortunately they did not pay for this favour, and the cost of feeding travellers could be quite a problem. In 1336 the abbot of Margam was forced to write to the main abbey committee in France, the Chapter General of the Cistercians, to complain that his monastery was always 'over-run with rich and poor strangers'.

Another group who lived apart from the monks, but this time within the abbey walls, was the lay brothers. The lay brothers had their own refectory and dormitory, and were expected to attend services in the church. They wore brown robes and were allowed to have beards. These lay brothers worked for the monks on their granges or farms.

They did not always behave like monks, however. In 1206 the abbot of Margam had to

The miraculous harvest at Margam Abbey

write to the Chapter General to ask for their advice. His letter reads like this:

'This year the lay brothers have rebelled against us at Margam. They chased me, the abbot, for fifteen miles away from the monastery. They threw my cellarer (who was in charge of the abbey's food and drink) off his horse. They then stopped the monks from having food and locked themselves in their dormitory.'

The Chapter General advised that the lay brothers should be separated from one another at once, and that no new ones should be allowed to join the monastery. Unfortunately we don't know the lay brothers' side of the story. We must remember, too, that the abbots only wrote to the Chapter General when something had gone wrong. There aren't any letters, for us to read today, which describe all the good things the monks did.

There was plenty of work for lay brothers at a monastery like Margam. They could help with digging for coal, or they could fish on the river Afan nearby. Later, when there weren't enough lay brothers, the monks allowed local people to fish the rivers and to pay them a rent. The rent for fishing the river Afan was 17 salmon, 40 sewin and 4 gillings for a year.

The most important work was looking after the huge flocks of sheep the abbey owned. Margam kept 5 245 sheep at one time, for meat and wool. The Cistercians became more and more wealthy, as they became better farmers and landlords. Walter Map, a writer from Hereford, noticed that a gap was growing between the white monks and the Welsh people. He said, 'The Cistercians have many coats, the Welsh none; they have boots and shoes, the Welsh go barefoot'. Would this kind of wealth have made it difficult for the white monks to keep to the rules of the Cistercian order?

A Pilgrimage to St Winifred's Well

This is a picture of pilgrims at Lourdes in France in modern times. Pilgrims are people who travel long distances to worship God and the saints at a holy shrine or church. Some make pilgrimages because they hope to be cured of an illness or disease. Some go to prove that they are sorry for doing something wrong, and others look upon a pilgrimage as an adventure.

If you look carefully at the picture you will notice that many of the pilgrims are in wheelchairs. Three million pilgrims visit Lourdes every year and 50,000 of them are sick in some way. They come to Lourdes because they have heard the story of St Bernadette, the fourteen-year-old girl who thought she saw and spoke to the Virgin Mary, Mother of Jesus. The pilgrims also hope to see some miracle happen at Lourdes and the sick hope they will be made to feel better. The church at Lourdes was built especially for these pilgrims. It is underground and can hold 20,000 people.

There are also places in Wales where pilgrims have travelled on pilgrimages for many years. Almost every church and abbey in the Middle Ages tried to prove that it had some relic or remains of a saint. Valle Crucis abbey in Powys claimed to have a statue of Christ that could speak, and people used to flock to the monastery to see this miracle. The holy island of Bardsey was particularly popular. Pilgrims were willing to suffer the difficult boat journey to the island in order to visit the graves of the 20,000 Welsh saints who were buried there. One poet, Deio ab Ieuan, protested very loudly that all the abbot of Bardsey gave him for his effort was a meal of bread, cheese and buttermilk.

One of the most important Welsh pilgrimages throughout the Middle Ages was to the well of St Winifred at Holywell, Clwyd. St Winifred's life-story tells us that she lived in about the year 650 and that she was a royal princess. One day a prince called Caradog attacked her and killed her by cutting off her head. But her uncle, St Beuno, brought her back to life again. The crimson mark of the sword that killed her could be seen on her neck for the rest of her life. On the spot where she was killed a spring of water appeared. People believed it to be holy water and they

Bathers in the healing waters of the Piscina, Holywell, about 1890

began to travel from all parts of North Wales to pray and worship at St Winifred's well. The well's fame spread, and it was believed that both people and animals could be cured by the miraculous water.

Unfortunately, although this is a good story, we cannot depend too much upon it. St Winifred's life-story was not written down until about 500 years after her death. Most of it was made up by the story-teller. But we can be certain that her well became more and more popular as a centre for pilgrimages. In 1240, the shrine of St Winifred was put into the care of the white monks of the Cistercian abbey of Basingwerk nearby. The monks soon realised that they could make a fair amount of money out of the pilgrims who came to bathe in the holy water. They placed a box in front of the statue of St Winifred and the pilgrims gave gifts of money and even cows and oxen to the monks. Early in the fifteenth century the King of England himself, Henry V, walked all the way from Shrewsbury to Holywell to worship at the well. Poets, like Tudur Aled, described some of the scenes amongst the sick and crippled:

They throw their two crutches
. into her waters,
Then they jump up and down before her,
She gives help to the deaf
To the dumb she gives speech . . .

The beautiful well building and chapel which can be seen at Holywell today were built around 1500. Even when most of the other shrines and relics in Wales were destroyed by King Henry VIII a few years later, St Winifred's well remained as popular with pilgrims and sick people as ever. It is not surprising that it came to be counted amongst the seven wonders of Wales.

The Preaching Friars

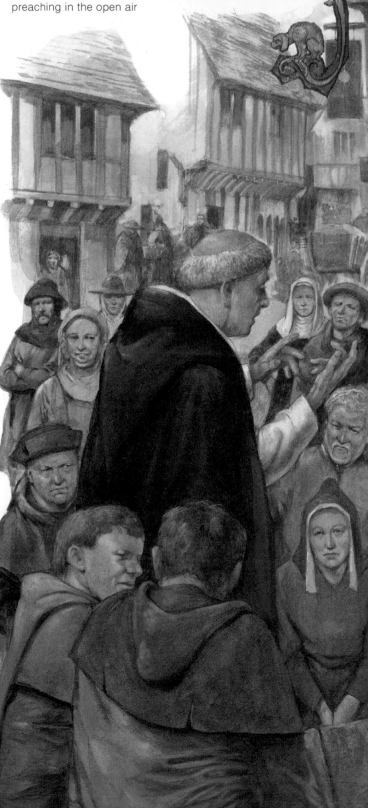

A black Dominican friar preaching in the open air

Let's go back about seven hundred years to a small Welsh town called Cardiff in South Wales. On the corner of a dark, narrow street a crowd has gathered to listen to someone preaching in Welsh. He looks like a black monk because he is wearing a black mantle over his long white robe. Yet the black Benedictine monks shut themselves away in monasteries, and did not go around preaching in the open air. Perhaps if we listen to his sermon we shall learn more about him.

'Brothers and Sisters', he says, 'I call upon you to come forward to confess to me all the evil things you have done during your lives. Have you tried to steal someone else's land, or have you been greedy for money and belongings? And what about the women here? Do you worry about how you look all the time? Don't forget that beauty fades away with old age. Let us remember the words Christ used: "Do not store up treasure for yourself on earth. Do not ask anxiously 'What are we to eat?' 'What are we to drink?' 'What are we to wear?' Each day has troubles enough of its own."'

The crowd stares at him in silence. The people have never heard anyone speak to them like this before. They can understand his language and his message, not like the services in church, where everything is in Latin. Yet he is not a priest or a monk. Who is he?

This preacher was, in fact, a black friar who followed the teaching of St Dominic of Spain. These preaching friars wanted to change things in the Church and the world, so they went out to meet the people and to teach them in their own language. Many of them were excellent scholars. The parish priests did not like them because they were afraid they would lose their jobs if the people began to go to the friars to confess their sins. A group of black friars opened their friary at Cardiff in 1241.

A few years later, another type of friar came to settle in Cardiff. These friars were followers of St Francis of Assisi, and they were so poor that they looked like beggars. Francis himself had been the son of a very wealthy shopkeeper but he decided to throw away his riches and become a friar. He wandered around the countryside preaching about God's love and peace. Soon others began to copy him and his fame spread throughout Europe and eventually to Wales.

St Francis's followers were called grey friars because of their coarse, rough grey robes, tied at the waist with a piece of rope. They walked barefoot and under their robes they often wore hairshirts, vests of rough goat's hair. This made sure that they could not lead an easy, comfortable life. One of the grey friars' rules was that 'every friar has to go out to beg for bread from door to door at least twice a year'. In Wales these friars were very popular at first. One of them, Madog ap Gwallter, wrote the first Welsh carol to teach people the true meaning of Christmas. In it he describes the baby Jesus as a:

> Great giant, small and frail,
> So mighty yet so weak, with cheek
>   how pale,
> So rich, so poor is he,
> Our Father – Brother . .

St Francis of Assisi helping a poor man

After some years, however, the friars, like the monks, began to gather land and possessions. Some people even began to argue with them about their sermons. A famous Welsh poet, Dafydd ap Gwilym, refused to listen to them. He said he would go on writing poetry about beautiful women. He argued that God would not have made beautiful women if he didn't want poets to enjoy and praise their beauty.

We mustn't forget that even if the friars' early enthusiasm and leadership cooled after a while, in the thirteenth century when they came to Wales their preaching and poverty was an example to others. It made people sit up and think about what being a member of the Christian Church really meant.

Gerald the Welshman – Bishop of St Davids?

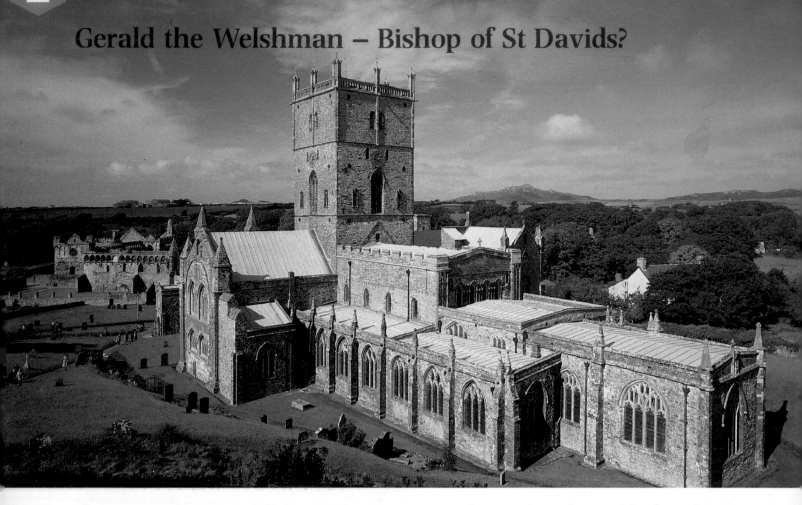

Look at this picture of the cathedral church of St Davids in Dyfed. It has always been an important church for Welsh people because St David, the patron saint of Wales, founded it himself. It was even said that two pilgrimages to St Davids were worth one pilgrimage to Rome.

It is hardly surprising that some church-men wanted to make St Davids even more important. They wanted it to become the main cathedral church of Wales, with an arch-bishop at its head instead of just a bishop, so that St Davids would be as important in Wales as Canterbury was in England. One of those who fought hard for St Davids to have a special place in the Norman Church was a remarkable priest, called sometimes Gerald de Barry, sometimes Gerallt Gymro (Gerald the Welshman) and sometimes by his Latin name Giraldus Cambrensis. But since Gerald was such a good speaker and lively writer, we can follow his story through his own words.

'Yes, I had always wanted to become Bishop of St Davids and to make it into Wales's main cathedral church. Even as a small child, when my three older brothers built sand-castles in the sand on Manorbier beach, I much preferred to build sand churches or sand monasteries. And my father, the great Norman baron, William de Barry, used to tease me and call me Bishop Gerald.

'Then I was sent to the right schools. I learnt to read and write Latin at St Davids itself, because my uncle was the bishop there. By the time I had finished my studies at the University of Paris, I had grown into a tall, good-looking young man, in spite of my huge bushy eyebrows. When I returned to Wales in 1174 I was ready for any challenge.

'My first job was to study the Church in

Wales and change anything that was wrong. I soon tackled those people who weren't paying their tithe money to the Church, and stopped the priests using cider instead of proper wine during the communion service. And when I found that the Archdeacon of Brecon, an important churchman, next in command to the Bishop of St Davids, kept a wife, against the rules of the Church, I had him thrown out of his job. I became archdeacon in his place.

'Yes, all seemed to be going well for me in my career, and I was very hopeful that I would be chosen as bishop after my uncle sadly died in 1176. But no, it was not to be. Apparently King Henry II went into a rage when he heard that my name had been put forward. What had I done wrong? I can only think that it was because I was part Welsh that the Normans didn't like me. To the Normans I was Gerallt Gymro, the Welshman, son of Angharad and grandson of the beautiful Nest, royal princess of Deheubarth. Because of my Welsh blood they didn't trust me. They knew that if I was made Bishop of St Davids I would try to make it equal to Canterbury. The Normans seemed to forget that I was really Gerald de Barry, three-quarters Norman, and proud of it! I felt very bitter indeed when they chose another Norman, Peter de Leia, as bishop. I was very jealous when he began to rebuild the beautiful old cathedral church!'

Poor Gerald. He could never understand why neither the Normans nor the Welsh would accept him. He was too Welsh for the Normans and too Norman for the Welsh.

About twenty years later when Peter de Leia died, Gerald tried once again to become Bishop of St Davids. He even travelled three times to Rome to argue his case. But he failed. He spent the rest of his life writing the books for which he has become so famous. So perhaps it was lucky for Wales that he didn't become a bishop or archbishop after all.

But Gerald's fight for St Davids was never forgotten. Many centuries later, in 1920, the Welsh Church did break away from Canterbury and was given its own archbishop. Perhaps Gerald had not fought in vain, after all.

(*above*) Henry II from an illuminated manuscript
(*left*) A statue of Gerald in St Davids Cathedral
(*right*) A present-day cartoon of Gerald with a tithe cow. Everyone owed the church a tenth of what they produced on their farm each year
(*below*) Gerald's family tree

RHYS AP TEWDWR

GRUFFUDD = GWENLLIAN   NEST = GERALD DE WINDSOR

LORD RHYS   DAVID FITZGERALD   ANGHARAD = WILLIAM
             Bishop of St Davids   DE BARRY

                                  GERALD

Gerald's Journey Through Wales

An archer from Gwent

One day, in the second week of March 1188, a large crowd gathered at Usk Castle, Gwent. Everyone was excited as they had heard that an important party of travellers was coming to Usk from Abergavenny. Some of them felt a little frightened too, because, amongst the crowd, there were several well-known local thieves and bandits. Why had they come? Were they going to rob and raid the travellers?

Soon a group of horsemen appeared over the brow of the hill and came to a stop by the castle. They looked peaceful enough, and as the crowd pressed forward, the people recognised one of the riders, the good and honest William, Bishop of Llandaff. An even more important bishop, it seemed, was about to talk to them. He began to speak in Latin, and no one could understand him. But the people need not have worried; his speech was being translated into Welsh and Norman French, and the crowd listened quietly. Let's join it, to hear what is being said.

'I, Archbishop Baldwin of Canterbury', translates the Welsh-speaker, 'have come to Wales to ask you to join me on a great journey, a crusade to the Holy Land. Last year, that dreadful monster Saladin the Turk captured the Holy City of Jerusalem from us, the Christian people. Men of Gwent, will you come and help us to recapture the most important city in the world? Will you take the Cross today?'.

'Huh', shouts a very rough-looking bandit in the crowd, 'What's in it for us?'. The crowd gasps. The people are afraid there's going to be trouble. But Baldwin is quite calm.

'There could be a good deal in it for you', he says, 'because if you join the crusade all the bad things you have done in the past will be forgotten, and you will not be punished for them. If you take the Cross you will be sure of a place in Heaven when you die'.

'But what can we do to help, Your Holiness?', shouts another.

'You men of Gwent are the best archers in England and Wales', replies Baldwin, 'Your rough elm bows will be excellent in the battles against the Turks.' A murmur runs through the crowd. They are obviously pleased by the Archbishop's praise.

'I'm prepared to help win back the Holy City of Jerusalem', shouts out a young man, 'But what do I have to do? How do I take the Cross?'.

'That's easy', answers Baldwin, 'Come forward to give your name, my son, and you will have a red cross to sew on to your cloak to show that you are a true crusader. And God bless you'.

Many others, including the bandits, followed the young man's example and took the Cross that day at Usk. Indeed, Archbishop Baldwin managed to recruit about 3,000 Welshmen to join the crusade on his journey through Wales, though many changed their minds later as they were persuaded by friends and relatives not to go on such a dangerous journey.

We know a great deal about Baldwin's tour in 1188 because Gerald the Welshman, or Giraldus Cambrensis, was a member of the party. He had been asked to join it because he knew Wales, the Welsh people and their rulers so well. Baldwin also expected him to help with the preaching and to keep a diary of everything that happened on the journey.

But Gerald was fascinated by all kinds of things – like the stories he heard and the local wonders he saw on his travels. He kept detailed notes of everything. Through his words we can see that travelling itself was difficult and dangerous at this time. Gerald's packhorse, carrying his most valuable books, was almost drowned as they tried to cross the quicksands at the mouth of the river Neath. They also found Merioneth, with its pointed crags and high mountains, to be 'the wildest and most terrifying region' in all Wales.

During the journey, Gerald loved to listen to stories about famous Welsh heroes and heroines such as Lord Ifor Bach of Senghennydd and the Princess Gwenllian of Kidwelly. He also found time to linger at Cenarth falls, Dyfed, to marvel at the leaping salmon in the river Teifi. Gerald, it seems, was quite right when he claimed that his book *Journey Through Wales* was 'like a highly polished mirror' reflecting much of the life and history of the Wales of his time.

Part of an illuminated manuscript showing Richard I fighting Saladin

Gerald's Description of Wales

A modern statue of Gerald of Wales

Have you ever wondered how you would describe Wales and its people to a total stranger? Would you describe the scenery – the mountains, rivers and beautiful beaches, perhaps? Would you mention the Welsh language or would you be happy with the picture of Welsh choirs and rugby players? It would be difficult to know what to put in and what to leave out. And how true and correct would your description be? After all, it would be your own personal view and someone else might have a very different picture of Wales.

These must have been some of the questions that faced Gerald eight hundred years ago when he decided to write his *Description of Wales*, to go with his famous *Journey Through Wales*. He saw Wales as one country and Welsh people as different and separate from the Normans and the English. Because he wanted to be fair to everyone, he divided his book into two parts, one to describe the good points and the other the bad points of Wales and the Welsh.

Gerald found plenty to praise in Wales. He noticed how fruitful some of the land was. He claimed that all the cattle and sheep in Wales

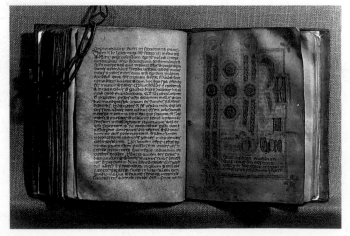

A chained book in a medieval library

could find pasture on the mountains of Snowdonia. Anglesey on the other hand was important for its wheat, and it was not surprising that the Welsh called the island '*Môn Mam Cymru*' (Anglesey, the Mother of Wales).

On his travels through Wales Gerald had been greatly impressed by the warm welcome he received everywhere. Indeed guests, even strangers, were very well treated. 'Those who arrive in the morning', he wrote, 'are entertained till evening with the conversation of young women and the music of the harp . . . In the evening, when no more guests are expected, the meal is prepared . . . The host and hostess stand up . . . and take no food until all the company is satisfied'. After the meal the Welsh loved to sing together in harmony, to talk about poetry or discuss relatives and families.

The Welsh were also determined to defend their way of life. If they were called upon suddenly to fight for their country they would drop everything and go as they were, dressed only in thin cloaks and barefoot, into battle. They considered it shameful to die quietly in bed, but a great honour to die fighting on the battlefield. But Gerald was not blind to the faults of the Welsh, either. He accused them of refusing to stand their ground in a battle. Instead, they would flee away on foot and hide in the woodlands, returning at night to attack the enemy through treachery. As he said, 'It is easy to beat them in a single battle, but very difficult indeed to win a war against them.'

Gerald felt that another weakness was the custom of dividing out land on a father's death, between all his sons. This led to fighting and bloodshed within families as they fought for the best land.

Gerald ended his description with two very different chapters. One told the Normans how they could finish conquering Wales by fighting the Welsh on foot, and building strong castles to keep them in their place. The other advised the Welsh how to defend themselves from the Normans. Gerald urged them to come together under the leadership of one good Welsh prince. If they did so, he was sure that such a strong warlike people could never be totally defeated.

But on whose side was Gerald, three-quarters Norman and one-quarter Welsh? We are kept guessing until the end, though there may be clues on the very last page. Here he told how King Henry II on one of his campaigns stopped to speak to one of his Welsh soldiers – an old man from Pencader, Dyfed. 'Who will win this war?' asked Henry and the old man replied:

'My Lord King, this nation may be weakened and almost destroyed by your soldiers yet it will never disappear altogether through the anger of Man, unless God is angry with it too … no other people, but the Welsh themselves, and no other language but the Welsh language, will have to answer to God on the last Day of Judgement, for this corner of the earth'.

The Welsh national football squad, 1990

Mountain scenery in Snowdonia

A Welsh language rally in Cardiff, 1989

Pontarddulais male-voice choir

The Fight for Independence and the Edwardian Conquest

Lord Rhys ap Gruffudd and Dinefwr Castle

(*above*) Dinefwr Castle before and after renovation
(*right*) Part of the song of praise to Lord Rhys

These pictures show part of Dinefwr Castle near Llandeilo in Dyfed, before and after it was restored. It will take about fifteen years for Cadw, the society which looks after historic buildings in Wales, to finish the work completely. The workers have to remove all the ivy from the walls and make the stones safe once more. When the work is completed, visitors will be able to enjoy the ruins of the medieval Welsh castle and imagine what life must have been like there over eight hundred years ago.

Why has Cadw decided to spend so much time in restoring Dinefwr Castle? After all, as we have seen, there are plenty of other splendid castles in Wales. The answer must lie in the fact that it played an important part in Welsh history, for it was probably built by one of the Welsh kings of Deheubarth. Later it was the home of one of the most powerful leaders in Wales – Lord Rhys ap Gruffudd of Deheubarth.

When Lord Rhys died in 1197, the scribe who kept account of every year and its happenings in the book called *The Chronicle of the Princes*, or *Brut* in Welsh, praised him very highly. Rhys had been 'the head, the shield and the strength of the south and of all Wales'. In peacetime he was generous, but in times of war 'like a bear growling or a lion attacking, his fierce anger raged against his enemies'.

The Chronicle tells the story of Wales from the year 682 until 1282. It describes many important Welsh leaders, but the song of praise to Lord Rhys is the longest and most colourful in the book. This does seem to suggest, doesn't it, that Rhys was a very special leader?

But it would be wise to remember that the *Chronicle* was probably written by the monks of Strata Florida abbey, and that Lord Rhys had given this abbey a great deal of land. The monks had good reason to praise such a generous patron.

Another writer who lived at this time and was related to Rhys was Gerald de Barry. Gerald also describes Rhys as a strong and powerful lord of Deheubarth. Rhys came to meet Archbishop Baldwin as he crossed from England into Wales at Radnor, to make sure that the Archbishop knew who was the most important Welsh leader in South Wales.

Rhys had worked hard to arrive at this high position of authority. On the death of his father Gruffudd, and his mother the brave Gwenllian, when he was only a child, the only land he inherited was the small commote of

Caio in Dyfed. Very soon he began to fight against the lords who had stolen his land. At this time, the *Chronicle* tells us, the French, Normans, Saxons, Flemings and Welsh were fighting against Rhys ap Gruffudd.

Soon Henry II, King of England, joined in the fighting too. He managed to capture Rhys and throw him into prison. Henry then decided that he would like to conquer Dinefwr Castle, and he sent a knight to find out more about it. A Welsh priest, Gwion, was chosen to show him the way. The knight asked Gwion to take him to Dinefwr by the most pleasant route. But Gwion was a crafty man. He led the knight along the most difficult and dangerous paths. As he went he picked up handfuls of grass and ate them. The knight was amazed. He returned to Henry's court and told him not to bother with Dinefwr. The people of the area ate grass like animals and it was a horrible place to live. The trick worked. Rhys was set free and Dinefwr was safe.

King Henry tried again, a few years later, to conquer the Welsh in battle, but this time all the princes of Wales from Gwynedd and Powys, and Lord Rhys of Deheubarth, rose up together against him. They didn't have to fight, however, because on the way in mid-Wales, Henry and his army were beaten by a hurricane of wind and rain and they decided to return home.

After this King Henry was too busy with other troubles in Ireland and in the Church to worry about Wales. He had shown Rhys who was the stronger by making him drop the title of King and use the title Lord instead. At the same time, since he wanted peace in Wales, Henry was willing for Rhys to become the most powerful leader in South Wales, to call himself Lord Rhys ap Gruffudd of Deheubarth and to rule his lordship from his castle at Dinefwr.

Lord Rhys's tomb in St Davids Cathedral

Story-telling at Lord Rhys's Hall

Iestyn ap Dafydd crossed the bridge over the river Teifi into Cardigan. In front of him he could see the two towers of Lord Rhys's new castle in west Deheubarth. Iestyn had visited the court at Dinefwr Castle several times but what kind of welcome would he receive here?

He need not have worried. Although Lord Rhys was now justicar or chief servant for King Henry II in South Wales and had begun to dress like a Norman and copy some of their ways, he was still a Welshman at heart. It was only last year, in 1176, that he had held a special feast for poets and musicians at Cardigan Castle. It had been announced throughout Wales, Scotland, Ireland and England a whole year in advance. Someone from Gwynedd had won the chair for poetry but there was great celebration when one of Rhys's own court won the chair for string music.

Iestyn ap Dafydd was not a poet or musician. He was a story-teller, travelling from court to hall throughout Wales entertaining the people with his collection of marvellous legends and stories. He was very popular because without him dark winter evenings could be long and boring.

Iestyn had decided that since he was at Cardigan Castle he would tell the legend of Pwyll, Prince of Dyfed. It would remind them of their Celtic past and the fabulous history of Dyfed, but it would also mention things like feasting and hunting boar and deer, with which they were familiar.

Most of them knew the story well. They had heard other famous story-tellers reciting it. Iestyn hoped he could remember every detail. He did not have a book to read it from, but knew it from memory. Tonight he would have to perform at his best, bringing the story and characters alive to his audience.

Let's join Iestyn in the hall at Cardigan Castle to hear about Pwyll, Prince of Dyfed. Iestyn is in the middle of his story. Pwyll has fallen in love with the beautiful Rhiannon but in a rash moment has promised his rival Gwawl fab Clud that he can marry Rhiannon. The two lovers hatch up a plot. Rhiannon will hold a feast for Gwawl. Pwyll will come to it dressed as a poor beggar and carrying a special bag. Listen to Iestyn telling the story.

'God bless you, beggar', says Gwawl, 'and welcome'.

'Lord', says Pwyll, 'I have come to ask you a favour because I am so poor. May I have a bagful of food?'.

'Of course, you don't ask much', replies Gwawl. 'Men, bring him food'. And so a number of servants brought food and began to fill the bag. But try as they might, the bag seemed as empty as ever.

'Friend', asks Gwawl, 'will your bag never be full?'.

'Not until a wealthy nobleman stands in the bag and says so', answers Pwyll.

'Here's a noble lord', says Rhiannon to Gwawl, 'Get up at once and stand in the bag'.

'All right', he answers.

And Gwawl gets up and puts his feet in the bag. Pwyll turns the bag until Gwawl is in it over his head. He ties a knot at the top, and blows his horn.

At once Pwyll's soldiers run in and capture Gwawl's men. As the soldiers come in, each one kicks the bag and asks, 'What have we here?' The others answer:

'A badger in a bag'.

Here we must leave the legend of Pwyll, Prince of Dyfed. Everyone seems to be enjoying the story, especially since they have seen beggars like Pwyll calling at the court. Most of them have played the cruel sport of baiting a badger in a bag, too. At about this time someone, no one knows who, wrote down these popular legends. They are known as the tales of the Mabinogi and because of their beauty and magic have become famous, not only in Wales, but throughout Europe and the world.

Lord Ifor Bach of Senghennydd Strikes Back

The year is 1158. Ifor Bach, Welsh Lord of Senghennydd, tells his wife Nest that he intends to attack the great Norman Lord of Glamorgan, William Earl of Gloucester, at his home in Cardiff Castle.

Gerald de Barry tells us this story – Lord Ifor Bach not only recovered his land but won a little extra land, too. But it was a short-lived victory. Within fifty years the powerful Clare family were Lords of Glamorgan. By 1268 Ifor Bach's great-grandson, Gruffudd ap Rhys, had been arrested and put in prison, and Gilbert de Clare was building his huge castle at Caerffili to show the Welsh that he was the new Lord of Senghennydd and Glamorgan.

The Doctors of Myddfai

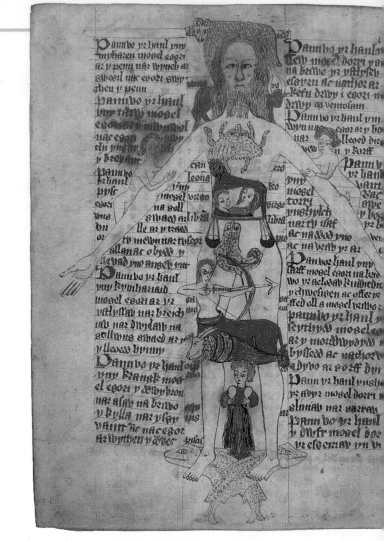

A page from a medieval medical book

Eight hundred years ago, if you had been bitten by a snake, wounded in a fierce battle or were just suffering from a painful toothache, and if you had lived near the parish of Myddfai in Dyfed, you would have been able to visit one of the famous doctors of Myddfai to ask for help.

These doctors were Rhiwallon and his three sons, Cadwgan, Gruffudd and Einion. They were the court doctors of Rhys Gryg, Lord of Dinefwr. To thank them for looking after his family's health Rhys gave them land on one of his manors in Myddfai. Even today, two farms in the area remind us of this important family of doctors. The names of the farms are Llwyn Ifan Feddyg (the Grove of Ifan the Doctor) and Llwyn Meredydd Feddyg (the Grove of Meredydd the Doctor). Since Rhiwallon and his sons were paid by their lord they may well have helped the poorer sick people, who could not afford to pay for treatment, for nothing.

There were probably other doctors in Wales at this time but we don't know anything about them. Luckily Rhiwallon's family wanted to share their cures and remedies with other people, and so they wrote them down. Several copies of their work have been kept for us today. The earliest copy is safe in the British Library in London.

What kind of medicines and cures would Rhiwallon and his sons have offered to the sick people at this time? Many of them were made from herbs and plants growing in the hedgerows and gardens of Myddfai. The doctors would grind the herbs hard with a pestle in a small bowl called a mortar. They would hang other herbs upside-down to dry over winter. They could add boiling water to these

herbs to make a herbal drink, or mix them with plant oil to make ointments.

If a patient had a swelling in his spine, for example, he would be advised to use a mixture made from grinding the root of the golden celandine flower and mixing it with a herb called fennel, some garlic, some vinegar or wine and some butter. This mixture would be placed on a cloth and wrapped around the patient's neck. The swelling and the pain would soon be better, claimed Rhiwallon.

Some of the recipes the doctors used seem very strange to us today. Look at the cure for a rotting wound, when gangrene was eating away the healthy flesh:

'Take a black toad which is only able to crawl and beat it with a stick until it becomes furious and so that it swells until it dies, and take it and put it into an earthenware cooking pot and close the lid on it so that the smoke cannot escape nor the air get into it, and burn it in the pot until it is ashes and put the ashes on the gangrene'.

This remedy sounds more like a witch-doctor's medicine than the work of a Welsh court doctor!

Medicinal herbs used in medieval times

Rhiwallon and his sons also studied the stars to help them find cures for their patients. They said that the movement of the planets told them what they should eat and drink every month of the year. In August they advised their patients to eat plenty of cawl (broth) and vegetables, and to put white pepper in their cawl. They should not drink beer or mead during this month.

These early doctors were also interested in preventing people from becoming ill in the first place. Their advice sounds like good common sense, even today:

'In summer, bathe in cold water ... then dress in fine clothes, because everyone feels happier in fine clothes and his heart is lighter. After that clean your teeth with the bark of dry hazel so that they will be brighter. You will speak more clearly and your breath will smell more sweetly.'

But where did these doctors of Myddfai learn all of this? Some stories claim that Rhiwallon was the son of the mysterious Lady of Llyn y Fan Fach lake, who reappeared from the lake to teach him all about the magic of plants and herbs. Others say that at this time there were many doctors in Europe using the same kind of medicines, experimenting with herbs and watching the stars. What do you think?

Llywelyn the Great and Joan

Alexander the Great of Macedonia, Catherine the Great of Russia, Alfred the Great of England; these are some of the rulers who have earned for themselves the title 'Great'. But what does a king or a prince have to do, to deserve to be called 'Great'? Only two Welsh leaders have won this kind of praise. One was Rhodri Mawr, King of Gwynedd, who conquered much of Wales and drove back the fierce Viking invaders. The other was Llywelyn Fawr, who lived in the thirteenth century. Let's find out why Llywelyn became such a popular and important leader in Wales.

Three huge problems faced Prince Llywelyn when he was given charge of his father's lands in Nanconwy, Gwynedd in about 1195. The first problem was to do with his own family and with the other Welsh princes of Wales. Through his cunning and strength as a soldier, he managed to defeat his uncles and cousins to become lord over the whole of Gwynedd. Because of this, most of the other princes of South Wales came to recognise him as their leader too, and to accept him as their lord.

The second problem Llywelyn had to face was King John of England. King John did not want to see a powerful prince ruling in Gwynedd. Llywelyn tried to tackle this problem in many ways. He married King John's daughter Joan, who must have found the simple court at Aberffraw very different from the dazzling London palaces she was used to. Joan was to become very important to Llywelyn. Within a few years her father and her husband were at war with one another. John attacked North Wales and the Welsh were forced back to the mountains of Snowdonia. In despair Llywelyn asked Joan to go to talk to her father for him.

The terms John demanded were very harsh. Llywelyn was forced to hand back many lands to the king; to give him 30 young hostages, including his own son Gruffudd; to pay the cost of the war with 20,000 cattle; and, of course, to pay homage to John as the main king. Joan did persuade her father, however, to allow Llywelyn to keep Snowdonia and his title as prince.

Now King John's attention was drawn away from Wales by his troubles in England. The Pope, King Phillip of France and John's own barons were against him. John was a cruel and unpopular king. In 1215 he was forced to sign the famous document called the Magna Carta. This document was the first step towards putting some control on the power of the King of England.

The stone coffin of Joan, Llywelyn the Great's wife, in Beaumaris church

then and Cardigan. Llywelyn did try other ways, rather than fighting, to live in peace with his Marcher neighbours. He gave his four daughters – Helen, Gwladus, Margaret and Gwenllian – to be married into important Marcher families and his son, Dafydd, married the daughter of William de Braose, Lord of Brecon, Builth and Abergavenny. In this clever way Llywelyn made sure that the Marcher lords would not wish to fight him.

Unfortunately for Llywelyn, sometime during these marriage talks his own wife Joan fell in love with the young Lord of Brecon, William de Braose. Llywelyn found out and in his anger threw Joan into prison. William suffered the most awful death for a lord, for he was hanged in public like a common thief. This proves that Llywelyn had become so powerful that he no longer cared what the Marcher lords thought of him.

This is how Llywelyn managed to solve the three main problems which faced him as a young prince in Gwynedd. Forty years later he could claim to be the main ruler in Wales and to call himself 'Prince of Aberffraw and Lord of Snowdon'. His wisdom, bravery and leadership so impressed the people of Wales that they gave him the title 'Llywelyn the Great'.

What was Llywelyn doing during these times of trouble in England? It's easy to guess. He was busy working with other Welsh princes, to win back all the lands and castles they had lost to King John and his Norman lords. The *Chronicle of the Princes* or *Brut* in Welsh, records their success with delight, and how they returned 'pleased and happy' to their own countries. Although Llywelyn did have several other clashes with King John and his successor Henry III, these did not lead to serious problems during the rest of his reign.

The third problem Llywelyn had to cope with was the power and strength of the Marcher lords who surrounded the Welsh kingdoms in Wales. The Earl of Pembroke, William Marshall, proved to be too strong for Llywelyn, by capturing the two castles of Carmar-

Statue of Llywelyn the Great in the square at Conwy

49

3

Llywelyn the Great's Last Years

A stone head, thought to show Llewelyn ab Iorweth

It is the nineteenth of October, 1238. We are in Strata Florida Abbey, in the middle of Dyfed. Strata Florida is a typical Cistercian abbey, where the white monks go about their work, worshipping in the beautiful abbey church, caring for the sick and the poor, farming their huge flocks of sheep on the abbey granges and reading and copying manuscripts in the peace of the monastery. Indeed, it is one of the manuscripts written by the monks of Strata Florida, the *Brut* or *Chronicle of the Princes*, which tells us what happened at the abbey on this very special day.

The abbey is full of visitors. Llywelyn ab Iorwerth, Prince of Aberffraw and Lord of Snowdon, has called together all the princes of Wales for an important meeting. Llywelyn the Great has been the main Prince of Wales for

about thirty-five years, but today he looks ill and old. Last year was a sad one for him. His wife Joan died, and he himself suffered an illness which has left him partly paralysed. Everyone seems so solemn. We'll ask one of the court clerks to explain what's going on.

'Llywelyn has called all the princes of Wales together, to get them to pay homage to his son Dafydd', he begins. 'He wants them to promise that they will support Dafydd as the main Prince of Wales after his death. Llywelyn has worked so hard for his title and his position. He's determined that his son shall carry on his good work.'

'*Hasn't he left it a bit late?*', we ask. '*Shouldn't he have thought of this before?*'

'But he has', assures the clerk. 'He's worked for this all his life. He's already made sure the King of England and the Pope accept his plan. He's also arranged for Dafydd to marry the daughter of the most important lord in the Marches. In fact, this is the second time he's called the Welsh princes together to promise their support.'

'*What's the problem, then? He seems to have done everything he can*', we say.

'I'm not quite sure', answers the clerk, 'but after his illness Llywelyn seems to be desperately worried about Dafydd and his country's future. His main adviser, Ednyfed Fychan, probably suggested this meeting, to show Llywelyn that everyone is backing him'.

'*And if Dafydd is Llywelyn's only son, he's bound to take over his father's title and position as the main Prince of Wales*', we argue.

'Ah – but that's the point. Dafydd is not Llywelyn's only son and heir. Llywelyn has two sons – Gruffudd and Dafydd. As you know Dafydd is Llywelyn's son by Joan, daughter of John, King of England. But Llywelyn had a son called Gruffudd by a Welshwoman, Tangwystl, before he married Joan. Llywelyn and Tangwystl were never properly married.'

'*If his parents weren't married, then Gruffudd won't count, will he,*' we say, '*even though he's older than Dafydd?*'.

'Yes, he will', answers the clerk. 'In the laws of Wales, all sons are treated in the same way and each one has the right to an equal share of his father's titles and lands when he dies'.

'*If that's the Welsh law, Llywelyn should stick to it. After all – he is the Prince of Gwynedd and the main Prince of Wales*', we venture.

'I know, but Gruffudd is a little bit wild and very Welsh, of course', explains the clerk. 'Dafydd has better connections with the King of England and the Marcher lords.'

'*That doesn't seem to be very fair, all the same*', we reply. '*Why didn't Gruffudd come here today, to fight for his rights before Llywelyn?*'

'There's little chance of that', says the clerk quietly. 'Dafydd and Gruffudd aren't friends at all, and when Dafydd gets into power – I pity his elder brother. He'll be thrown into prison, or even killed.'

We look quickly at the clerk's face. Does he support Gruffudd, the Welshwoman's son, against Dafydd? Could this be why Llywelyn the Great has gone to so much trouble to make the princes promise once again to support and be faithful to his son Dafydd when he dies? Will they keep those promises? Only time will tell.

The ruins of Strata Florida Abbey

A Hostage in the Tower of London

The word hostage is very familiar to us today. We hear on the news of people being taken as hostages when an aeroplane is hijacked. In some countries, important and influential people are kidnapped as hostages. They are held prisoner so that the different groups of enemies can use them when they are bargaining with one another.

Taking and keeping people hostage has been going on for centuries. In the history of Wales we remember how Henry II, King of England, set out in 1165 to conquer the Welsh princes and lords. He had to turn back, because of a hurricane. In his anger, the king ordered the twenty-two Welsh hostages in his care to be cruelly beaten and have their limbs broken. He was so furious with Lord Rhys that he ordered his son, Maredudd, to be blinded with a red-hot poker. Because of his blindness, Maredudd had to spend the rest of his life as a monk in the Cistercian abbey of Whitland in Dyfed.

Prince Gruffudd, the son of Llywelyn the Great, must have remembered these terrible stories about hostages as he paced to and fro in his prison at the Tower of London in 1244. To make matters worse, he had been handed over as hostage to the King of England by his own half-brother, Dafydd. Gruffudd wasn't too sure what Henry III hoped to do with him. Could he trust Henry when he said he might help Gruffudd to return to Wales, to recapture his land and title from Dafydd? He didn't really think so.

Gruffudd had to admit that life in the Tower was not too miserable. After all, his

The Tower of London
(*left*) during the Middle Ages; (*above*) today

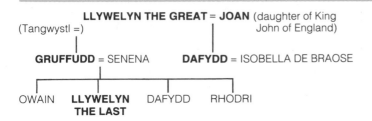

Welsh wife, Senena, and his children were allowed to visit him. His room was well furnished, with curtains and plenty of bedclothes. Yet he was tired of being used like a pawn in a game of chess in the talks between Dafydd and the king.

As he looked back, it seemed to Gruffudd that he had spent far too much of his short life behind prison bars. The first time he had been taken hostage he was only eleven years old. His father Llywelyn had fallen out with the King of England, and he'd been forced to hand over his own son to the King. Gruffudd had been a hostage for four years.

When he was set free, Llywelyn tried to be fair to him by giving him lordships and lands. But Llywelyn had also begun to show that Dafydd, Joan's son, was going to be his heir. Gruffudd became more and more jealous of Dafydd, and he began to behave in a wild and headstrong way. At last, when Llywelyn could bear no more of his trouble-making, he threw Gruffudd into prison for six years in Degannwy Castle in 1228.

It isn't surprising that Gruffudd ap Llywelyn should have felt so bitter on that fateful night in 1244. He and his son Owain had been prisoners of Henry III in London for three long years, and there was very little hope of being set free for many more years. Gruffudd wanted to be back home in Gwynedd, arguing and fighting for his fair share of his father's lands and titles. He felt it was his duty to claim his lands for his sons, especially as Dafydd had no sons of his own yet. As he thought of his four sons – poor Owain, a prisoner with his father; the daring Llywelyn who was proving to be a skilful warrior; and his two youngest sons Dafydd and Rhodri – Gruffudd knew that he must do something at once.

He knew what he had to do. He had to escape. Carefully he knotted the bedclothes and curtains into a long rope, and lowered it out of the window. He glanced down at the ground below and shuddered. Then he climbed out and began to descend slowly, his plump, heavy body straining the hand-made rope. Suddenly the bedclothes ripped, the rope snapped and Gruffudd fell from the keep in the Tower of London to his death.

It was the early hours of 1 March, St David's Day. It seemed as if Gruffudd ap Llywelyn's hopes of winning back the crown of Gwynedd for his own family had been dashed forever.

Gruffudd ap Llywelyn falling to his death from the Tower of London in 1244

At the Ford in Montgomery

This is a picture of Pope Adrian V, one of the most important churchmen in the world in the second half of the thirteenth century. Yet, before he became a pope, and when he was called by the name Cardinal Ottobuono, this man played a leading role in a dramatic event in the history of Wales.

On 29 September 1267 Cardinal Ottobuono was with a group of people at a ford, crossing the river Severn, near the castle of Montgomery in Powys. Nearby stood Henry III, the King of England, and his young warrior son, Edward. On the other side, and preparing to cross the ford was Llywelyn ap Gruffudd, grandson of Llywelyn the Great. At last, thought Ottobuono, his task in Britain was almost over.

Ottobuono had been sent to Britain by the Pope to try to sort out the problems between the English king, his barons and lords, and the princes of Wales. When the main rebel baron, Simon de Montfort, had been killed in battle in 1265, the troubles between Henry III and his English lords had come to an end. But Llywelyn of Wales was still a thorn in Henry's flesh. Llywelyn had used the wars between the English barons and the king to win back all the lands and titles his uncle Dafydd ap Llywelyn had lost to the king when Llywelyn the Great died in 1240.

Nothing was allowed to stand in Llywelyn's way. He threw his brothers into prison and made himself the new Lord of Snowdon. Before long his authority stretched down to Deheubarth, Brecon and Abergavenny in the south, over into Powys in the east and all along the north coast of Wales. When Henry III came to Wales to try to control this ambitious prince, Llywelyn moved all the women, children and cattle out of their homes into the mountains in Snowdonia. Henry was forced to give up his campaign. He found that the mountains of Snowdonia were like a huge castle protecting its people. Even when he managed to get over one range of mountains, another one faced him. The people couldn't be starved out of their mountain castle either, because there was plenty of food and grain on the island of Angelsey – 'the mother of Wales'.

Because of all his successes, the Welsh people began to look on Llywelyn as their natural leader and he was given the title of 'Prince of Wales'. In fact, he was so popular with his people at this time, that one lord grumbled that men followed Llywelyn as if they were glued to him.

Ottobuono watched as Llywelyn crossed the ford to pay his homage to the King of England. Llywelyn went up to Henry and knelt before him. He lifted up his hands and Henry clasped them in his own. This meant that Llywelyn accepted Henry III as the main King of England and Wales, and that he promised to be loyal and faithful to him. In return, as Ottobuono had promised Llywelyn, Henry would accept that Llywelyn was the 'Prince of Wales' and that most of the other Welsh princes would, from now on, pay homage to Llywelyn and not to Henry III. This was the first time an English king had ever accepted the title of Prince of Wales. Henry had even agreed that the title could be carried on by Llywelyn's son and heir after his death. No wonder Llywelyn II, Prince of Wales, looked so proud. He knew that this must be the most important day of his life.

Ottobuono wrote to the Pope about this meeting. He said:

'The people of England and Wales have been quarelling for a long time, both have suffered in turn ... God has looked upon them with mercy and wishing in these days to end their suffering he has led them ... to an agreement!'.

This agreement was called the Treaty of Montgomery. It seemed to promise a new time of peace between the old enemies in England and Wales.

But Ottobuono must have known in his heart that all the problems had not been solved completely. Llywelyn was going to have to pay 25,000 marks for this peace. How could he raise such a huge sum of money without straining his poor people to the limit? He was also concerned about ambitious Prince Edward. He felt sure that Edward, once he became king, would never allow Llywelyn to remain as Prince of Wales. And what of the future? Llywelyn was not even married yet and had no son and heir. What would happen if the Prince of Wales died suddenly without an heir? Wales could lose its independence and freedom overnight.

One of the parliaments of Edward I of England. Llywelyn of Wales is seated to Edward's left, and Alexander III of Scotland to his right

Death at Cilmeri, 1282

A modern memorial to Llywelyn near Cilmeri

'And then Llywelyn was betrayed in the belfry at Bangor by his own men.' This short sentence must be one of the most irritating ones in the *Chronicle of the Princes*, or *Brut* in Welsh. What exactly happened in the bell-tower of Bangor cathedral? Why should his own men have turned against the Prince of Wales, Llywelyn ap Gruffudd? Were they, perhaps, tired of trying to raise more and more money for him to pay off his debts to the King of England? Had Llywelyn become a hard and cruel leader? We shall never know the answers to these questions, but we do know that within months, Llywelyn, Prince of Wales had been betrayed. He was killed in an ambush in Cilmeri, mid-Wales.

There are several different versions of Llywelyn's last days and once again we shall never know exactly what happened on the fatal day of 11 December, 1282.

By this time the powerful warrior Edward I was King of England. Edward had been determined, from the beginning, to squash Llywelyn. Through the years he had managed to push him further and further back into the mountains of Snowdonia. Yet Llywelyn still used the title 'Prince of Wales', much to Edward's annoyance.

Then suddenly in 1282, a fierce war broke out between Dafydd, Llywelyn's brother, and Edward I. Llywelyn was forced to join in, to support his younger brother. King Edward gathered a huge army and planned his campaign. It was to cost over £60,000. He sent out three armies – one to attack North Wales, one to attack mid-Wales and one to attack South Wales.

Llywelyn was busy for some time fighting the king's army in North Wales. Then he made rather a strange move. He travelled to Builth in mid-Wales to help defend the river Irfon near Cilmeri against the royal army. Somehow, during the fighting, Llywelyn found himself cut off from the rest of his army. Suddenly his small band of faithful warriors was surrounded by English knights. One of them (a knight called Stephen de Frankton according to one

version of the story) ran his lance through Llywelyn's body and killed him.

One or two of the writers who have chronicled this happening suggest that Llywelyn had been tricked. After all, what was he doing in mid-Wales at all, so far from his own land in Snowdonia? How did he become separated from his own troops in such a dangerous area? These are some of the mysteries still surrounding the death of Llywelyn ap Gruffudd in 1282.

As soon as the English knights realised the prize they had taken, they cut off Llywelyn's head. Edward ordered it to be taken at once to London, and to be paraded on a pole through the city streets. Then it was to be placed on display at the Tower of London where his father Gruffudd had died so tragically over forty years before. But the white monks of

Llywelyn's grave at Cwm-hir abbey

Cwm-hir abbey near Cilmeri remained faithful to their prince. They asked permission for his body to be buried at their abbey, and today a beautiful modern stone marks his lonely grave.

Soon after, Llywelyn's brother Dafydd was also betrayed 'by men of his own tongue' and was cruelly executed by Edward I. Llywelyn's only child and heir, a baby daughter called Gwenllian, was taken away to spend the rest of her life as a nun in England.

Yet even if there are so many confusing and mysterious aspects to Llywelyn's last days, there can be no doubt about how some of the Welsh people felt at this tragedy. The words of the poet Gruffudd ab yr Ynad Coch are famous today. He tells us that it was as if the whole world had come an end. Heaven itself turned against Wales, he says. He asks in despair:

'Don't you see the way of the wind
    and the rain?
Don't you see the oak trees beating
    against one another?
Why, O my God, does the sea not cover
    the land?
Why are we left to linger?'

The Welsh believed that Llywelyn ap Gruffudd, Prince of Wales, would be the last truly Welsh prince of his country. In 1282, as the *Chronicle of the Princes* says, it seemed to many that 'all Wales was cast to the ground'.

Edward the Conqueror

The ruins of Rhuddlan Castle, Clwyd

When King Edward I of England announced his Statute of Wales at Rhuddlan Castle in March 1284, he must have felt a tired but proud man.

He would have been tired because his war against the great Welsh rebels, Llywelyn ap Gruffudd and his brother Dafydd, had been a long and hard one. The Welsh had been a thorn in Edward's flesh for over ten years. Seven years earlier he had forced Llywelyn back into the mountains of Snowdonia. Now he had defeated him completely. Edward was worried that the wars had cost him so much money. In 1282 alone he spent £150,000 (about £100 million today). This was more than he could hope to raise through taxes in a year, and the drain on food and men had been difficult to bear.

But Edward would also have been proud of his achievements. He could claim to be Edward the Conqueror, the king who had taken over Wales, just as William the Conqueror of Normandy had taken over England in 1066.

Now Edward realised that he needed a detailed plan to make sure he kept his hold over his new principality. He decided to divide Llywelyn's Gwynedd into three counties, Anglesey, Caernarfon and Merioneth. He created a new county of Flintshire in the lands near Chester, and in the south-west he turned the old Welsh lordships into the counties of Carmarthenshire and Cardiganshire. Edward would have felt even prouder if he had known that these new counties would last for almost seven hundred years.

In the new counties Edward appointed special officers: a chief justice each for North and South Wales, and a sheriff for every county. In this way he could make sure that his own men would fill the most important jobs in Wales to keep an eye on the troublesome Welsh people. Edward also decided that the old Welsh laws dealing with murder, stealing and arson couldn't be used any longer. English laws would take their place.

Yet Edward would have known quite well that his power as a king only covered one part of Wales. Much of the country, along the border with England and down into Glamorgan, Gwent and Pembroke, still belonged firmly to the great Marcher lords. Even Edward the Conqueror had not beaten the whole of Wales.

Edward realised too that sheriffs and justices would not be enough if the Welsh people began to rebel and revolt. After the war with Llywelyn in 1277, Edward had decided to build strong stone castles all around the Welsh principality. He had worked hard and spent a great deal of money building and rebuilding the castles at Aberystwyth, Flint, Builth and Rhuddlan. Now, seven years later, to prove that his conquest was final, he began a massive programme of castle-building at Conwy, Caernarfon, Harlech, and later at Beaumaris.

Around the castles special towns were set up, where only English men and women could live and work. Even though the castles were different in shape and design, they all played an important part in Edward's masterplan. If a serious revolt broke out, the people in the castles could not be starved out in a siege because the castles were built on rivers or on the coast. They were built to last and they are the best evidence we have today of King Edward's plan to conquer Wales completely. If we can imagine these superb castles as they would have looked in the Middle Ages, with their huge walls covered in whitewash, we can understand why the Welsh people, living in the surrounding countryside, feared and hated them so much.

Many important Welsh people must have decided at this time that it was pointless to try to fight against Edward any more. They decided to come over to his side, and to prove their loyalty they presented him with the most valuable relic in Gwynedd, a piece of Christ's cross. This was taken to London and paraded through the city by the king and queen, and their nobles. Edward also took Prince Llywelyn's golden coronet back with him to Westminster in London.

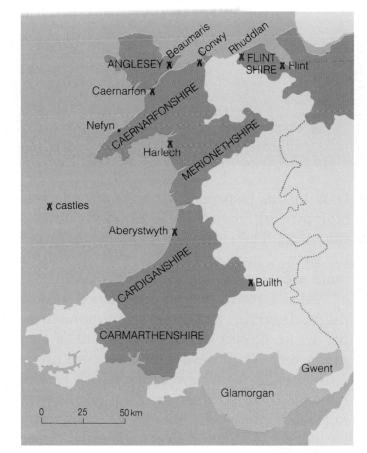

Edward I's castles in Wales

After setting out his plans for his new principality, King Edward decided to celebrate his great victory with a royal tournament. This was to be held at Nefyn in Gwynedd. Nefyn had been one of Llywelyn's most important courts, and now it was Edward's. Then Edward set out to march in triumph all around Wales, through his new counties and the Marcher lordships, to prove once and for all to the Welsh people that he was their new king and conqueror.

Conwy – Building a Castle

Look at this picture of the magnificent castle built by King Edward I of England at Conwy in Gwynedd. The castle stands at the mouth of the rivers Conwy and Gyffin, and it guards the main route from England along the north coast of Wales. Edward was so determined to build his castle on this particular spot that he threw the white monks of Aberconwy out of their monastery. They were forced to move up the Conwy valley to a new abbey which Edward built for them at Maenan. King Edward was not too fond of the monks of Aberconwy, because they had always supported Prince Llywelyn and the Welsh cause.

Let's take a walk through Conwy Castle to find out how it was built. It must have been very difficult, in the old days, to get into the castle at all. You would have had to climb up a steep stairway, cross a drawbridge over a deep chasm, and then walk through three gateways. It isn't surprising that Welsh rebels only managed to capture this castle through treachery. During Owain Glyn Dŵr's revolt, a hundred years after the castle was built, a carpenter betrayed its soldiers while they were attending a service in the church, and the rebels managed to enter the castle grounds.

Once inside the castle we notice the eight tall towers, four on each side. These were built in two rows, to fit on to the rock on which the castle stands. There are turrets, or small extra towers, on four of the large towers to show that this was a royal castle. King Edward and his queen, Eleanor, must have spent some time at Conwy Castle. They had their own special rooms on the first floor. They would have joined in the services in the beautiful little chapel, and danced and feasted in the Great Hall.

By 1287 the building work was finished and the famous architect, Master James of St George, could sit back proudly to examine his work. Let's ask Master James to tell us about the building of Conwy Castle.

'We've almost finished here at Conwy, thank goodness', he says. 'My craftsmen have worked very hard. I never thought we'd be able to build such a huge castle in so short a time. It's only taken us four years, and you've got to remember that we have to stop working in winter when the weather is too cold or wet. I must admit that Conwy Castle has come along faster than any of the other castles in Gwynedd. Look at Harlech. We've still got another two years' work there at least, and I don't know when we'll finish at Caernarfon. I've chosen a very special design for Caernarfon Castle. The walls will have bands of stones in different colours, to make them look like the walls of the city of Constantinople.'

'I suppose you've noticed', he continues, 'that Caernarfon and Conwy are quite similar. They're both surrounded by borough towns. I've had to design walls to go around these towns too, to stop the Welsh people moving in. You should walk around Conwy's town walls to see the twenty-two towers we've built in them, and perhaps you'll also notice the row of twelve garderobes, or toilets. These are useful for our soldiers when they're on duty. All these castles and towns are going to cost King Edward a great deal of money. Conwy Castle alone has cost £15,000. I've tried to cut costs as much as possible, but as soon as my back is turned it's spend, spend, spend.'

Master James of St George is in his element talking about his castles. His story goes on:

'These Welsh castles have been quite a challenge for me. Of course, my father was a master builder back home in Savoy on the borders between France and Switzerland, but I was very flattered when King Edward asked me to be the master of his works in North Wales. He offered me a very good salary too, the huge sum of three shillings a day for the rest of my life! He was even willing to pay 1s 6d a day as a pension to my wife Ambrosia, if anything should happen to me. Now I've passed on the family trade to my son Giles. He's busy at Harlech Castle at the moment. Perhaps one day we'll be able to repay King Edward for giving us so much work and money by building him the perfect castle. He's going to need strong stone castles in Wales, because the Welsh will always be Welsh and they're very ready to rise up in revolt. But, gentlemen and ladies, you must excuse me. There are still a few details to be cleared up, here at Conwy.'

(*left*) A stone carving from Salisbury Cathedral showing builders at work and (*below*) A plan of Conwy Castle

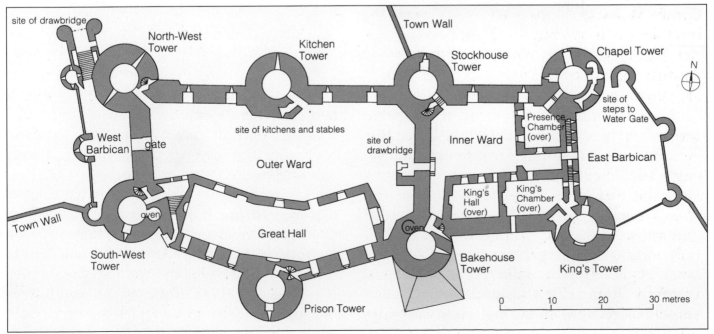

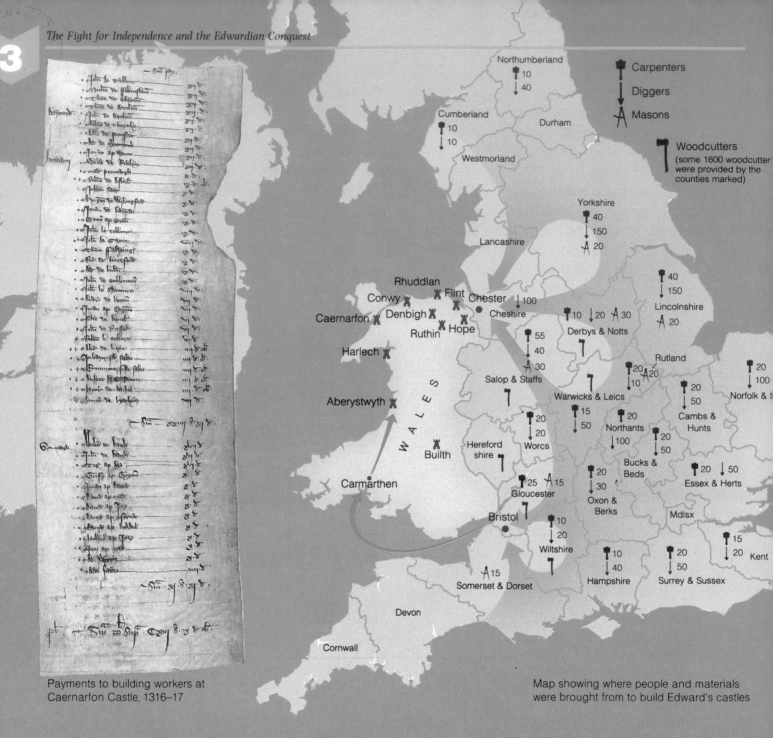

Payments to building workers at
Caernarfon Castle, 1316–17

Map showing where people and materials
were brought from to build Edward's castles

As Master James walks away, it is easy to understand how he came to be considered the greatest architect in the history of English castle-building. He designed and supervised the work at eight of King Edward's castles in Wales. He also realised his great dream of designing the perfect castle for Edward. In 1295 work began on Beaumaris Castle in Anglesey. He chose to build it to a concentric design, with one castle inside another. These round castles were so strong, they were impossible to conquer. Beaumaris Castle is the best concentric castle in Britain.

Our attention is now drawn from the great master-builder to his workmen and craftsmen. Edward I believed that 'many hands make light work', and he made sure that there were plenty of workers to finish the job. During the summer of 1286 alone over 950 men worked at Harlech Castle. Around us we see men and women labourers digging rubble and carrying stones. It is hard, back-breaking work, although there are some machines to help lift the very heavy loads. Nearby work a group of stonemasons and carpenters. They talk together in English. Where have they all come from? How did they get here, to Conwy? We'll have to find out.

'I'm from Lincoln in England. I was told that I had to come here to work for King Edward, to build his Welsh castles. There are 150 diggers, 40 carpenters and 20 stone-masons here from Lincolnshire. We were marched to Chester to meet up with other workmen from all over England. I suppose King Edward couldn't trust the Welsh to build castles for him. They would probably have refused, anyway. Guards kept watch over us for most of the journey, in case we tried to escape. Luckily the king had already sent gangs of woodcutters from all over England to fell the trees and clear paths for us, before we marched through Wales.'

'*What exactly is your work here at Conwy Castle?*' we ask.

'I'm a skilled stonemason. I have to carve and dress the best stones for the fireplaces and the windows. The best stone comes from Cheshire, but most of the stone for the walls is from local quarries.'

'*If you're skilled at your craft, you must be quite well paid,*' we venture.

'I suppose we can't really complain', he agrees. 'We get threepence a day as stone-masons, but the poor labourers who carry all the heavy wood, soil and stone only get eight-pence for a whole week.'

'*You must feel proud, now that the work is almost finished*', we say.

'Indeed I do. Conwy is a beautiful castle and I'm sure it will last for very, very many years.'

The walls of Conwy Castle today remind us of the craftsmen from all over England who were marched by King Edward to North Wales to build them. We're lucky that Edward paid clerks to keep detailed accounts of his castle-building in Wales. These accounts are kept safely at the Public Record Office in London.

Yet, in spite of all the money and time spent on these magnificent castles, they were not used often as royal palaces, and they were not

Medieval builders at work

put to the test many times by strong revolts. When Welsh rebels led by Madog ap Llywelyn attacked Conwy in the winter of 1294–5, King Edward himself was besieged at Conwy Castle. The siege continued for some months, and stocks of food and drink began to run out. According to a historian called Hemingburgh who lived at the time:

'He (Edward I) suffered for some time both hunger and thirst. He drank water mixed with honey and did not have enough bread to eat . . . Now, although they had only a little wine, hardly a flagon, the bottle which they had decided to save for the king, he himself was not willing to enjoy, but said, "In time of need all things must be shared equally, and we must all submit to the same diet until such time as God himself takes care of us in heaven".'

Soon, however, Edward had crushed the revolt and he left Conwy for England. It was because of this revolt that Edward decided to build Beaumaris Castle.

The castles built by King Edward were feared and hated by the Welsh people of his time. They represented conquest and the fail-ure of the Welsh people in their struggle for independence. Today, strangely enough, Welsh people are proud of Edward's castles. The castles attract many visitors to Wales, and the Welsh are able to profit from Edward the Conqueror's castle-building.

Llywelyn Bren Attacks Caerffili Castle

Llywelyn Bren, Lord of Senghennydd, laid siege to Caerffili Castle in Glamorgan in 1316. He claimed that he had 10,000 men on his side, but he soon realised that taking Caerffili Castle might be too much of a challenge even for them. What drove this Welsh lord to attempt this, and why were so many Welshmen willing to join him in rebellion?

Llywelyn, it seems, had very definite reasons for rising up in revolt. He must have known that his great-grandfather, the famous Lord Ifor Bach of Senghennydd, had taught the Normans a trick or two at Cardiff Castle. Yet since the conquest of Wales and the death of Llywelyn II in 1282, the Welsh lords of Glamorgan had lived in peace with the Norman families, and especially with the lords de Clare. Then, in 1314, young Gilbert de Clare, Earl of Gloucester and Lord of Glamorgan, was killed in a battle in Scotland. The cruel Payn de Turbeville was appointed by the king to look after Glamorgan for him.

De Turbeville had no time for the Welsh people. He was a hard master. He demanded more and more money and he took jobs away from the Welsh and gave them to his own people. Llywelyn Bren saw the suffering and despair, and decided to ride to London to ask for King Edward II's help. But the king was not interested in squabbles in faraway Glamorgan. As Llywelyn travelled home to Senghennydd, he was a bitter but determined man. He had heard that the Welsh were rioting already. Now he would not only join them, but as Lord of Senghennydd, he would lead them.

As he and his troops gathered outside the gateway of Caerffili Castle, Llywelyn must have wondered whether he had made a huge mistake. The castle looked massive. It was the largest in Wales, built by the de Clare family fifty years earlier. The Norman lord had wanted his castle to be a strong fortress. He had chosen to build one castle inside another in a concentric design. The large lakes surrounding the castle also helped to defend it. An enemy soldier might just manage to cross the first lake and climb the great outer wall of the castle. But once inside, he would be faced with another lake and the strong inner castle.

Llywelyn's first plan must have been to try to surround the castle completely with his men, so that no fresh food could reach those inside. But the castle site with its lakes covered 12 hectares, and Llywelyn soon realised that this would be an impossible task.

Next he could have turned to the special machines built at this time for attacking castles. There were giant catapult machines which could throw stones, heavy arrows or the bodies of dead animals or even enemy soldiers over the moat to batter against the stone walls to try to destroy them. Sometimes soldiers hurled 'Greek fire', a liquid containing naphtha, from these catapults. This burning liquid would strike the wooden buildings and thatched roofs of the cottages inside the castle, and soon everything would go up in flames. But poor Llywelyn could see that these machines were useless against Caerffili Castle. The stones and arrows would never reach the great stone walls. Siege ladders or covered wheeled platforms, called mantelets, could not be used either, because of the lake.

It isn't surprising that after nine long weeks, Llywelyn Bren had to give up his siege of Caerffili Castle. According to one chronicler there were, in fact, only three people defending the inner castle against him. They were Lady de Clare herself and two servants! They must have been very glad indeed that the defences of Caerffili Castle were so strong.

By now, King Edward II had called upon armies from west and east Wales to destroy Llywelyn's rebellion. As these large forces marched towards Caerffili, Llywelyn knew he had lost his fight. He and his men were forced to flee to the caves in the mountains. He must have been a brave man, for he decided to give himself up to Lord de Bohun and his army. Llywelyn said to him, 'It is better that one man should die than that a whole people should be killed'.

As he was a traitor, Llywelyn Bren's lands and belongings were handed over to the Crown. It is interesting to look at the list of his belongings, because it shows what kind of things a Welsh lord owned at this time. Amongst them we see one coat of mail, one pair of metal gloves, one gold brooch, eight books (three of them in Welsh), ten gold rings, three Welsh chairs and many other valuable possessions.

Llywelyn Bren was punished severely for daring to lead a revolt, and for trying to capture the great castle at Caerffili. As a warning to other rebels, he was dragged through the streets of Cardiff and then taken to be hanged, drawn and quartered.

Llywelyn Bren being dragged through Cardiff

Life in the Borough Towns

In the shadows of his mighty castles, Edward the Conqueror built special towns or boroughs. These boroughs were an important part of Edward's masterplan, to show the Welsh people that he now ruled Llywelyn's lands. This wasn't a new idea – we've seen already how the Norman lords built castles and boroughs like Cardiff, Cydweli, Usk and Carmarthen when they first came to Wales, to control the local people. Now it was Edward's turn.

Gerald the Welshman said that in his time the Welsh people didn't like living together in towns or villages. They preferred to live in scattered homes in the countryside. A hundred years later, in Edward I's time, the Archbishop of Canterbury said the same thing when he visited Wales. In fact the Archbishop must have made a mistake, because by this time, when Llywelyn ruled Gwynedd, many Welsh people had moved to live in towns such as Nefyn, Caernarfon and Llan-faes in Anglesey.

Now Edward I wanted to control Llywelyn's Welsh towns, and to build his own English towns or boroughs around his new castles. To build these new towns he took land which belonged to Welsh people and gave it to settlers from England. Around the town of Denbigh in Clwyd he claimed 10,000 acres of the best land and gave it to people from Lancashire and Yorkshire. The local Welsh people were given 10,000 acres in return, but it was very poor land, up on the mountainside. You can imagine how bitter these Welsh people must have felt.

How did King Edward manage to attract people from England to come and live in such a dangerous foreign country? If we visit the old Welsh town of Llan-faes in about the year 1301, we can find out what happened. Llan-faes was one of the largest towns in Llywelyn's time. It was a busy wine port and fishing centre. By the time of our visit, in 1301, it looks rather empty and desolate. We meet the local Welsh doctor, Master Einion, and ask him what's wrong.

'What's wrong? Can't you see what's happening here? Look over there and you can see King Edward's new castle at Beaumaris. It's only a mile away, and now he's brought English people to live in the new borough town. He's given this borough a royal charter. Our trade has been ruined here at Llan-faes, and soon our town will be destroyed.'

'*What is a charter?*', we ask.

A plan of Beaumaris drawn in 1610

'A charter gives the townspeople or burgesses very special rights and privileges. They can carry weapons to protect themselves against us, the Welsh. One of them acts as a watchman at night, and rings a bell every two hours to say that all is well. On top of that, Edward has given every burgess a piece of land called a burgage. The burgess doesn't have to pay rent on this for ten years. Just imagine ten years without paying rent! Another annoying thing is that we, the Welsh, can only buy and sell our goods outside the new borough town walls. We even have to pay tolls for this favour. This makes us feel like outsiders in our own country. It's so unfair.'

'But if Beaumaris is growing so quickly, what will happen to you, the old burgesses of Llan-faes?', we enquire.

'I don't know. King Edward tells us that we can't move into Beaumaris, but we can move to a new borough he's built for us twelve miles away, at Newborough. Some people have already moved, but I'm not going. No one can force me to leave my home at Llan-faes', Master Einion replies firmly.

We know today that Master Einion, the doctor of Llan-faes, was fined for being so obstinate. He was forced to move eventually. We also know that Newborough developed into quite a large Welsh town. When Dafydd ap Gwilym, the famous poet, visited Newborough fifty years later, he was charmed by 'her wine, her people, her beer, her mead and her love'.

On the whole, the Welsh people hated Edward's new borough towns. The charters he gave them can still be seen today, and many of the towns are now very proud of them. But at the time, they caused great problems for the Welsh people. The English settlers were given all kinds of rights and privileges, while the Welsh lost their trading rights and lands. This caused bitterness and dislike which would soon erupt into hatred. During the following century, English burgesses and boroughs were often attacked by angry and frustrated Welsh outsiders.

The Black Death

Can you imagine a terrible disease gripping your family, your school, your village or your town and killing many of your relations, friends and neighbours? This is what happened in Wales in 1349, when the cruel plague called the Black Death swept through Britain. We can't be certain how many died. Some historians believe that one and a half million people, out of a population of four million, died in England alone. One Welsh writer at the time believed that half the people of Wales had died. We shall never know, because so many of those who collected this information also died of the disease.

There can be no doubt that the plague reached every corner of Wales. A lord's son at Abergavenny in Gwent died. All the tenants on Llan-llwch manor near Carmarthen were killed. In Rhuthun, North Wales, over 77 people died in one fortnight in June. How was this awful disease brought to Wales, and how did it kill so many people so quickly?

A black rat with one of its fleas magnified. The fleas carried a germ, *Pasteurella pestis*, which infected humans with the plague when they were bitten

The plague was, in fact, a disease infecting fleas that lived on black rats. The fleas moved to live on human beings. The fleas would bite humans and pass on the sickness. Then it would be passed from one person to another. The plague probably arrived in Europe from China, and it travelled into Wales from the port of Bristol.

Burying plague victims

A person suffering from the Black Death was a pitiful sight. He or she began to sneeze and soon his or her body, especially the armpits, was covered with horrid boils and black swellings. The flesh rotted away, and the smell was overwhelming. The fever lasted for only a few days. The person either recovered within three or four days, or died. The body of such a victim would turn black, and this is why the disease was called the 'Black Death'. The bodies had to be buried together in great pits, because there was no one left to make decent coffins for them.

What could people do, to try to protect themselves against this awful plague? The herbal books offered several suggestions:

'Take a fistful of sage, a fistful of rosemary and a fistful of feverfew. Wash them well and place them in a glass of Malmsey wine. Drink two silver spoonfuls of this mixture every day'.

People were also advised to prepare their homes by 'cleaning them well and burning brushwood indoors. Then disinfect the house with herbs'.

Once a patient caught the disease a doctor, if one could be found at all, could do little to help. Most were afraid to go too close to the patient in case they caught the plague themselves. Many people panicked. Husbands ran away and left their sick wives, and mothers abandoned their dying children. There was no known cure, and most people believed that the plague was God's way of punishing his wicked people. They met to pray for God's help and forgiveness. They even whipped and tortured themselves to show how sorry they were for their sins.

But what about the land? How did the Black Death affect life in the countryside in Wales? There was no one left to sow seeds and to care for the crops and animals. No one went to the fairs and markets. A report on the manor of Llanfair near Chepstow, Gwent, describes how even the dovecotes lay empty, for 'The doves are nesting in the hall and the other rooms in the manor'.

Procession of flagellants in 1349. Religious people sometimes whipped themselves as punishment for their sins in the hope that this would stop the plague from spreading

The landowners found that they did not have enough workers or bondmen left on their farms. In the Llanrhystud area of Dyfed only seven out of 104 workers survived the plague. Because there were so few workers, they could demand higher wages, shorter hours and better working conditions. Many bondmen ran away from their manors and became freemen on much higher pay in other parts of the country. Others were forced to work even harder by the landowners. They had to do the work of those who had died, as well as their own work. It was a time of great unrest and change in the Welsh countryside.

When summer turned to winter the plague died away slowly. But it came back to sweep through Wales several more times during the Middle Ages. We know of these later visits through poetry written at the time. Ieuan Gethin, a poet from Baglan in West Glamorgan, lost five of his children in one month. He names them – Sion, Ifan, Morfudd, Dafydd and Dyddgu – and he describes the boils, the size of ten pence pieces, which killed them. Another poet from North Wales lost ten children from the plague.

This cruel disease was to visit Britain again, with great force, in the seventeenth century. The last great outbreak occurred in China only a hundred years ago, and some people have died of it in England this century. Even today, doctors have no cure for the fearful 'Black Death'.

Dafydd ap Gwilym

Statue of Dafydd ap Gwilym

Have you heard the old saying that a sailor has a girlfriend in every port? It would seem to be true too, that Dafydd ap Gwilym, a well-known poet in the Middle Ages, had a sweetheart in every area of Wales. His poems are full of these girls. He names a few of them: Dyddgu with her beautiful black hair; Elen, an English businessman's wife; and his favourite, his 'lovely goddess' Morfudd, with her blonde hair and her jealous husband! He describes all these girls with such mischief and fun that his poems are still attractive to us today.

The troubles that were affecting Wales at this time are not important in Dafydd's poetry. He does not talk about the cruel black plague, the hardship and poverty or the revolts against the Norman and English boroughs. And yet Dafydd must have known about these problems. After all he was a nobleman, born at Brogynin near Aberystwyth. He used to go to church at Llanbadarn Fawr nearby. The English townspeople of Aberystwyth came to this church too, but Dafydd doesn't seem to worry about the troubles between the Welsh country folk and the English of the towns. Why? Because he is too busy studying the beautiful girls at the church service. Instead of facing to the front and listening to the priest, Dafydd stretches his neck to stare at his favourite girlfriend. The other girls laugh at him and mock his long curly hair. In spite of all his efforts, poor Dafydd fails to win any sweetheart at all.

Dafydd spent much of his youth at the house of his uncle, Llywelyn ap Gwilym. Llywelyn was the constable of Newcastle Emlyn castle in Dyfed and an important royal servant. He taught Dafydd everything a young lord should know: how to fight and ride, to hunt and hawk, to dance and play chess, to sing and write poetry. Then in 1343 Prince Edward of England sent an official to examine Llywelyn's work as a constable. He was thrown out of his job and a Norman, Richard de Vere, took his place. Soon tempers flared up between Llywelyn and Richard. They began to fight and Richard was stabbed to death. Although Dafydd doesn't mention this terrible tragedy in his poems, it does seem that he was forced to look for a new patron in another part of Wales at about this time. Was this why he spent so many years at generous Lord Ifor's court at Basaleg in Gwent?

Dafydd travelled from one end of Wales to the other during his life. He visited Cardiff, St Davids and Carmarthen in the south and Bangor, Caernarfon and Newborough in the north. Although he was Welsh he seems to have been quite at home in the new English borough towns and he was happy to praise

A bone chessman from Skenfrith Castle, Gwent, (*left*) and an ivory pawn from Caerleon Castle (*right*)

them. As he travelled, Dafydd loved to study the world of nature. His poems show his delight at the beauty he saw around him, in trees, woods, animals and birds. He describes the owl, the song-thrush and the holly bush in detail, and he sends the swan and the seagull, 'all one white with moon or snow', to carry messages of love to his many sweethearts. He tells the skylark to go to Gwynedd where 'a fair and talented maiden' lives and not to return without 'one of her kisses'.

The Foelas crwth, 1742, in the Welsh Folk Museum Collection

It isn't surprising that Dafydd loved the month of May. During the winter months he had to stand outside in the freezing cold for hours, serenading his girlfriend under her window. He was always half afraid that her husband might wake up suddenly and be very angry with him for trying to steal away his wife! But in the month of May he could meet his loved one outside under the cover of a leafy bush or tree. No one would be able to find their secret meeting place in the wood.

In these poems Dafydd is always poking fun at himself as the poor, unlucky lover. This love of fun and his delight at the world of nature made Dafydd's poems new and fresh in Wales in his time. We can still enjoy their beauty today, and it is not surprising that Dafydd ap Gwilym is considered by many to be the best Welsh poet ever.

Trouble at a Tavern

Dafydd ap Gwilym, the famous Welsh poet, and his young servant arrive at the borough town of Newborough in Anglesey. It is about the year 1360.

4

Women in the Middle Ages

This is a reconstruction of an early 15th-century kitchen. The lady of the manor is instructing the servants. What do you notice about the servants? Can you spot where the bread was baked and how the meat was roasted on a spit? Which items would you *not* find in a kitchen today? What kind of problems might you have had working in a medieval kitchen like this one? Women like this had to work very hard to run a big household when their husbands were away.

Look at this picture of women praying in the late Middle Ages. Look at their long flowing dresses and the high head-dresses with their sweeping trains. Pictures like this can tell us a great deal about women's fashions at this time, but they cannot tell us about their thoughts and their feelings. Indeed it is surprising how little we know today about how over half the population lived in the Middle Ages. In those days, women hardly ever wrote about themselves.

During the Middle Ages a young noble-woman had two choices in life: she could either marry, or become a nun. Girls would be promised in marriage at a very young age, sometimes when only six or seven years old. Joan was probably only ten when she married Llywelyn the Great, and Margaret Beaufort was only fourteen when she gave birth to the future King Henry VII. In England a marriage was supposed to last forever. In Wales husbands and wives could be separated if they wished. A wife could leave her husband if he was very ill or if he had bad breath. If they had been married for over seven years all their belongings had to be shared out equally and fairly. Animals, tools and furniture were divided. The husband's share of the animals would be the pigs, the hens and one cat, while the wife would have the rest of the cats, the sheep and the goats. Even the children were shared, with the father having the eldest and the youngest sons, and the mother the middle son.

Young girls who were unable to find husbands or who chose not to get married could become nuns. Welsh girls who wanted to become nuns could choose between a small nunnery at St Clears in Dyfed or the two Cistercian nunneries at Llanllŷr, Dyfed, and Llanllugan, Powys. Once again these girls joined the nunneries at a very young age and were expected to take their vows of poverty, purity and obedience before they were sixteen. When King Edward I of England finally defeated his old enemy Llywelyn the Last of Wales in 1282 he took Llywelyn's baby daughter Gwenllian and locked her up forever in a nunnery at Sempringham.

We can be sure that most Welsh women lived busy, full and useful lives in the Middle Ages. A noblewoman had to look after a large household, ordering the food, managing the money and instructing the servants as they prepared meals. A craftsman's wife was expected to help her husband at his craft, although she usually earned only half his pay for doing the same work. Women were not allowed to go to university or to become priests or doctors at this time. Most women could not read or write, of course.

The wife of a farmer, labourer, or one of the many poor people had to work extremely hard. Out in the fields she would gather stones, or weed and plant seeds, or harvest the crops. Around the farm or cottage she would milk the cows and tend to the pigs and hens. In the house she had to make bread, cheese and butter, cook all the meals, spin and weave cloth, wash and mend clothes as well as look after the children. It was difficult to be house-proud in a house shared with sheep and oxen. A woman's work was never done. It is hardly suprising that with so much work to do ordinary women had neither the time nor the patience to write about their life in the Middle Ages.

Owain of the Red Hand

Let your imagination take you back to the port of Harfleur in Normandy, France, in the year 1372. There are soldiers everywhere, preparing to board a fleet of sailing ships. There is excitement in the air, and as we listen we can hear people speaking in French, Breton, Italian and even Welsh! Let's stop one of the Welsh soldiers and ask him what's going on.

'We're going on an expedition tomorrow, across the sea, back to Wales', he explains.

'But who are all these soldiers? Surely they're not all going to attack Wales?'

'Yes, they're going to help Owain Lawgoch, Owain of the Red Hand, to conquer Wales. He's the true Prince of Wales'.

'The true Prince of Wales? That's impossible, the last Welsh Prince of Wales was Llywelyn ap Gruffudd and he died at Cilmeri in 1282!'

'Ah! But Owain's full name is Owain ap Thomas ap Rhodri, and Rhodri was Llywelyn's brother. So you can see that Owain has every right to call himself Prince of Wales.

He's just been to Paris to tell everyone that he's going back to Wales to claim his lands and titles as Prince.'

'*Why should these French soldiers fight for Owain, though?*', we ask.

'The King of France, Charles V himself, is backing Owain. He's lent him ships and money. Charles would do anything to make life difficult for the King of England. They're always at war here in France because King Edward III of England claims that lands in Normandy, Anjou and Aquitaine in France belong to him.'

'*And what of the French soldiers?*'

'They think Owain is a superb soldier. Many of them have fought with him all over Europe. Perhaps it was because of his bravery in battle that he's known as Owain of the Red Hand. The French call him Yvain de Galles.'

'*What of the Welsh people? Do they support this man who's pretending to be their true prince?*'

'So we've heard. Perhaps the Welsh are getting tired of the English kings. Perhaps they've had enough of the heavy taxes used to pay for these wars. And the poets have been busy stirring things up, of course. One of them has just written a poem asking whether there is "a champion of Llywelyn's blood" who can come to save his country. I'm sure we'll have a warm welcome in Wales.'

With these words the soldier leaves us to sail out of Harfleur for Wales. Owain Lawgoch's ships sailed out into the Channel. But they never arrived in Wales. For some reason they stopped on Guernsey island. While they were there the King of France sent an urgent message to Owain, commanding him to return at once to help him. For the second time in his life Owain ap Thomas ap Rhodri had to leave the task of claiming his land and title in Wales unfinished. When he had set sail for Wales the first time, three years previously, rough stormy weather had forced him to turn back.

After this second failure Owain continued to serve the King of France, though he never forgot his dream of becoming the Prince of Wales. Welshmen came to join his company of 500 soldiers and many of them, like Ieuan Wyn, called 'the great lover' were colourful characters. One day a new soldier from Wales, called John Lamb, appeared in Owain's camp. He was Owain's constant companion as they tried to capture Mortagne Castle on the French coast. Then, as Owain sat one morning, Lamb came up behind him and stabbed him in the back with a dagger. Lamb received £20 from someone important in the English court for this murder. The court must have been very afraid of Owain to have arranged and paid for such an act. One poet cried out in despair, 'He (Owain) was killed, and it was a devil who killed him'.

Siege of Mortagne-sur-Mer showing Owain's death

This fascinating story of how the last true heir of Llywelyn ap Gruffudd tried to win back his title as Prince of Wales has been kept for us in the writings of a Frenchman called Froissart. He also records that Owain's body was taken to nearby St Leger church to be buried. But the people and poets of Wales would not allow their hero to die. Like King Arthur before him, Owain, they claimed, had not died at all. He was asleep in a cave in Dyfed somewhere, and he would return to save his country in its hour of need and to claim his title as the true Prince of Wales.

Sycharth – a Medieval Home

Have you noticed advertisements selling houses in a newspaper or in an estate agent's office? The descriptions praise the houses highly and emphasize all their good points. They don't mention, of course, the leaking roof or the rotting woodwork.

There weren't any estate agents in the Middle Ages, but we do have excellent descriptions of some important medieval homes. These were written by poets who tramped the countryside in search of a welcome. In a way these poets were like today's estate agents. They too emphasized the good points about a hall, a mansion or an abbey. This was their way of saying thank you for the welcome and the hospitality shown to them.

One of the most famous of these poems is Iolo Goch's description of the court at Sycharth, Powys. As the poem unfolds we can almost see the court before our eyes. From this

description the artist has tried to draw Sycharth as it would have appeared to Iolo Goch in 1385. It is a difficult task. How successful has the artist been?

As he approaches Sycharth, Iolo Goch sees a court standing high on top of a green mound. It is surrounded by a golden ring of water. Iolo walks over the bridge towards the gateway. The building reminds him of a church because it is in the shape of a cross and it has a bell-tower. It is built of wood, like so many of the other black and white houses that are popular along the border between England and Wales. As he looks up, Iolo sees the tiles on the roof and the high chimney 'which doesn't allow smoke to gather'. How different this court is from the home of an ordinary peasant with its mud walls and thatched roof, with only a hole for the smoke to escape.

The court, says Iolo, is made up of nine rooms or halls. The Welsh laws commanded the king's men to build their lord nine houses, including a hall, a bedroom, a kitchen, a chapel, a barn, a kiln, a stable, a beerhouse and a toilet. As the years passed, these nine halls, as at Sycharth, were brought into the same court. The stained-glass windows attract Iolo's attention too. Inside the rooms there are plenty of wardrobes to hold clothes, dishes and unusual foods and spices.

As Iolo takes us outside, he proudly points to the orchard, the vineyard, the parkland full of deer and the small park for rabbits. We notice the dovecot, the fish pond, the heronry and the lawns with their peacocks. A little further away we see the green meadows and the cornfields near to the corn mill where the corn will be ground into flour. Sycharth does seem to be a most delightful property, according to Iolo's description.

But Iolo also takes us to meet the family who live in this beautiful home. We join them for a meal in the hall and there is plenty of beer and wine, bread and meat for everyone. The hostess, Margaret, is the daughter of Sir David Hanmer, an important royal servant,

and is 'the best of all wives', according to Iolo. Everyone receives gifts at Sycharth. The door is never closed for there is,

'No hunger, disgrace or dearth,
Or even thirst at Sycharth.'

The head of this happy household is Owain Glyn Dŵr, who is descended from the princes of North Powys on his father's side and from the royal house of Deheubarth on his mother's. When he was young he studied law in London, joined the royal court and helped the King of England to fight against rebels in Scotland. Now, aged about thirty years, he feels ready to settle down to a comfortable family life in his splendid moated home at Sycharth.

Aerial view of the remains of Sycharth, Powys

Today there is nothing left of this medieval home. Within twenty years, Sycharth had been destroyed completely. In 1403, young Prince Henry was in the Shrewsbury area fighting against a rebel Welsh army being led by none other than Owain Glyn Dŵr himself. In a letter to his father, King Henry IV of England, he describes how he travelled to Sycharth and 'when we arrived there was not a soul around, and so we burnt the whole court to the ground'.

It is very fortunate for us today that Iolo Goch described this medieval Welsh court in such detail, before it was destroyed forever.

Owain Glyn Dŵr's Revolt

On 16 September 1400, Owain Glyn Dŵr rose up in rebellion against his neighbour, Reginald Grey, Lord of Rhuthun. With hundreds of men he attacked and burned the towns of north-east Wales. Owain had fallen out with Reginald Grey over some land. The King of England would not listen to his complaint because he was friends with Grey. When Owain tried to bring his case before the English parliament they had laughed and said, 'What do we care for these barefoot rascals?'.

But Owain was much more than just another Welsh rascal rebel. Before he had set out to attack Rhuthun, his followers had crowned him Prince of Wales. At once hundreds rushed to join his army. Most of Wales was up in arms.

Why were so many of the Welsh ready to support Owain Glyn Dŵr, to risk their lives to fight with this almost unknown Welsh Marcher lord? Why was Owain himself willing to leave his comfortable home and family at Sycharth to live the life of a rebel and outlaw? We shall try to find out the answers to these questions by interviewing some of his supporters.

The first person we ask is a Franciscan friar from Llan-faes in Anglesey. He has no doubts about backing Owain. 'The churchmen in Wales', he says, 'have had enough. All the friars and Cistercian monks I know are helping Glyn Dŵr. The abbot of Llantarnam even says he's going to fight in battle for him. We're all fed up with the king and his important servants trying to control the Church in Wales. Did you know that only one Welsh bishop is a Welshman? There's no chance at all of a Welshman getting any good job in the Welsh Church!'

'I know exactly how you feel, friar', says another supporter from Clynnog in Arfon. 'I'm just a small farmer and I've joined the rebellion because Owain is attacking the English borough towns in Wales. It isn't fair that the Englishmen in these boroughs stop us selling our goods as we want to. And do you

know that they have the cheek to call us "mere Welshmen" and "foreigners" in our own country? About twenty-five years ago my father and eight others from Clynnog were arrested for selling beer outside the walls of the borough town of Caernarfon. These have been cruel years for the Welsh!'.

'That's just what I said', agrees an elderly poet called Gruffudd Llwyd. 'This is a sorry world indeed. We, the poets of Wales, have been calling on Owain to rise up to save his country. After all he's got plenty of good royal blood in his body and he can claim to be the true Prince of Wales. At last he's listened to his people and they have answered his challenge!'

'We could hear his call as far away as Oxford University', adds a young Welsh student. 'As soon as we knew that a rebellion had broken out in Wales, we rushed home to join his army. As we came home we met Welshmen working in the harvest in England. They dropped their tools and came with us too. Things haven't been too happy for us, the Welsh students at Oxford, for some years now. Not long ago there was a riot against us, and the English students were shouting out "Kill, kill the Welsh dogs". I'm glad to be back home fighting for the Welsh cause.'

'I'm just glad to be back fighting', says Henry Don, a lively young nobleman from Dyfed. 'I enjoy a good war. I've just been fighting the enemy in France and Ireland and I'm looking forward to trying to capture Cydweli Castle for my new prince, Glyn Dŵr.'

All these supporters would not, of course, have gathered together in one place to fight for Owain Glyn Dŵr. Yet they were typical of those who did join in the revolt. It seemed to the English that 'all the Welsh nation except a few' were Glyn Dŵr's men. Whatever their different reasons for supporting him, they felt that he had come, as he claimed, 'to set the Welsh people free from our English enemies'. The local, personal quarrel between Owain Glyn Dŵr and Lord Grey of Rhuthun had turned into a national and popular revolt.

Owain Glyn Dŵr: Man or Magician?

Owain Glyn Dŵr's rebellion raged on from strength to strength for six years. He won two striking victories in battle, one at Hyddgen in Powys and the other at Bryn Glas in Gwent. He attacked castles from Brecon to Cardiff, Cydweli to Aberystwyth and Caernarfon to Harlech. Owain captured two important English lords. One was Reginald Grey, his old enemy. He made Grey's family pay the huge sum of 10,000 marks before he set his hostage free. The other lord was Edmund Mortimer, but this time Owain won his hostage over to his side by arranging for him to marry his daughter.

Such a war was bound to be fierce and cruel. Adam of Usk, who wrote a chronicle of these times, tells us how the leaders behaved. Owain and his Welsh chiefs were like 'outlaws, hiding, looting and killing their enemies'. The English king, Henry IV, burned and destroyed everything, too, as he and his army marched through Wales. They did not spare 'even children and churches, nor the monastery of Strata Florida. For they used the church and choir up to the altar as a stable. They took back with them to England over a thousand children, both boys and girls, to be their servants, and they left the whole place in ruins'. Poor Adam of Usk wasn't sure which side to support. He seems to have decided that the best plan would be to keep out of danger during the revolt.

Owain's fame spread outside Wales, too. He called upon the King of Scotland and the Irish lords to support him. Soldiers from Brittany and France sailed to Cydweli and Caernarfon to help, and one French army marched from Milford Haven in Dyfed right to Worcester in England to join Owain in battle. He also

This illustration of the Battle of Shrewsbury, 1403, when Hotspur son of the earl of Northumberland was killed, was probably drawn soon after the battle

made use of the quarrel between Henry IV and some of his most important noblemen. He joined with Edmund Mortimer, his son-in-law, and Percy the earl of Northumberland, in a plan to throw Henry IV off the English throne. Then they would divide England and Wales among the three of them. Mortimer would rule southern England, Northumberland would rule northern England and Glyn Dŵr would be Prince of a much larger Wales.

But Owain was not just another warrior prince. He wanted his country of Wales to have a parliament of its own, so he called his men together once at Machynlleth and then at Pennal in Gwynedd. At Pennal, Owain and his chief leaders put forward a new and exciting plan for the churchmen and scholars of Wales. They called for the Welsh Church to be cut off from Canterbury, to be independent with its own main cathedral at St Davids. They said that all priests in Wales should be able to speak Welsh, and they also talked of opening two universities, one in North, and one in South Wales. These ideas must have pleased the churchmen and the students who had joined the rebellion.

King Henry IV and his people couldn't understand how Owain Glyn Dŵr, the Welsh rebel, had become so popular and successful. Could he be some kind of magician? Holinshed, an English writer, said that very strange things had happened on the night Owain was born. He had heard that at that moment 'all Owain's father's horses in the stable were found standing in blood up to their bellies'. The English were rather afraid of Crach Ffinnant, Owain's personal poet and prophet, who always seemed to be at his side. All their worries were confirmed in 1402 when Henry IV led his army into Wales to conquer Owain once and for all. From the time when they

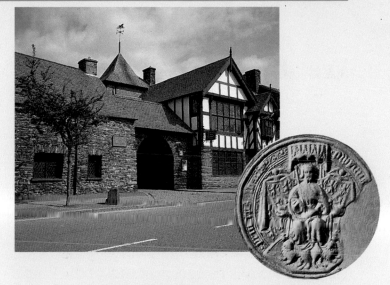
Owain Glyn Dŵr's seal and his parliament house at Machynlleth

entered Wales to the time they left, rain mixed with snow and hail made everyone very, very cold! Then came a hurricane of wind and rain to destroy the army's tents. The army had to turn back for England without fighting Glyn Dŵr at all. King Henry's historian was almost sure that Owain had used magic this time!

There must be many other reasons to explain Owain's success during these six years. He made some clever moves. He became friends with Henry IV's enemies in France, Scotland and England. He tried not to fight King Henry in proper battles, but to attack him by raiding here and there, using guerrilla tactics. He had excellent servants from among the churchmen and on the battlefield. But perhaps the most important reason was that Owain Glyn Dŵr was a natural leader. He was a prince of great dignity and he was never betrayed by his own men, even during the darkest days.

Before long the dark days did arrive. Owain lost control of his castles. He had no ships to carry food to his soldiers. His army of farmers went back to their harvests. Some stayed with him to the end. Owain would not accept a royal pardon. In 1415 he disappeared without trace. A Welsh chronicler says, 'Some say that he died, but the prophets say he is alive'. Certainly his dream of one united Wales still haunts Welshmen today.

Map showing the division of England and Wales into three parts

Welsh Soldiers Abroad

Among the thousands upon thousands of parchments and documents kept safely at the great Public Record Office in London is a list of names from the Carmarthen area, dated 20 June, 1415. It is written in a spiky brown hand, probably belonging to one of King Henry V's clerks in the Great Hall of the King's castle at Carmarthen. We can see that some of the men named on the list, Jenkyn ap Harry of Llansteffan or Philip ab Adda of Laugharne, were Welshmen, while others such as Thomas Cooke and Phillip Bennet were probably Englishmen who had moved into the area to live in the borough towns. But Welsh or English, these men are all listed as soldiers who joined King Henry's army to fight against the French in the great battle of Agincourt in France.

The battle of Agincourt from the St Alban's Chronicle

A battle axe

Why should these men have wanted to sign on to serve the King in his French campaign? Over 250 men from Carmarthenshire were willing to risk their lives to help Henry defeat the French. We can only suggest some reasons why they did this.

It is likely that many of the men listed had only just finished fighting against the King of England for their great hero Owain Glyn Dŵr. Perhaps they felt that they had nowhere to go and no work to return to. These men would have been attracted to join Henry's army by the good wages on offer. Rumour had spread that the King was offering foot archers 4d a day for the campaign. As ordinary farm workers, they couldn't hope to earn more than 1½d for a whole week's work. Changing sides and becoming one of the King's archers would certainly have seemed like a sensible idea.

Many of these men would also have become very experienced archers during the years of Glyn Dŵr's rebellion. King Henry recruited 5,000 archers into his army in 1415, and these masters of the longbow could kill even the powerful knights on their huge war horses. Seventy years before, at the battle of Crécy, the Welsh bowmen had helped to destroy the great French army of knights. On the morning after the battle 15,000 French soldiers lay dead, but only a hundred English and Welsh men had died. The best archers could release 15 arrows every minute, so that the sky itself seemed to turn black.

A sense of adventure and excitement would have attracted others to join the English army. They would have heard thrilling stories about other Welsh soldiers fighting elsewhere in Europe. They might know the story of Owain of the Red Hand, who had fought for the King of France against the English, and had tried to return as the true Prince of Wales to reconquer his father's land. Or they might be familiar with the blood-curdling exploits of the Welsh warrior Sir Hywel ap Gruffudd, and his fearsome battle-axe. According to a story recorded by Sir John Wynn of Gwydir several centuries later, Sir Hywel's battleaxe was so respected that it had a special place in the Prince's court, and a plate of food would be placed before it every day. Of course, the axe didn't eat the food! The ceremony shows how important Hywel's battleaxe had been in the French campaigns. After the meal, the food on the axe's plate was given to the poor.

The Welsh soldiers abroad had become famous for their rough and wild ways. One writer describes them on the way to battle:

'In the very depths of winter they were running around bare-legged. They would eat and drink anywhere ... They were great drinkers ... Their pay was too small and so ... they took things which did not belong to them!'.

It was probably because the Welsh soldiers were so unruly that the Prince had ordered, before the battle of Crécy in 1346, that they should all be dressed in the same way, with a hat and jacket of green and white. The green had to be worn on the right side.

As the soldiers in the Great Hall of Carmarthen Castle waited patiently to sign their names on the list of those to go 'with our most excellent lord the King on his journey to France', these thoughts of adventure, wealth and excitement must have gone through their minds. Few of them knew, or cared, why the King of England kept fighting the King of France. It must have seemed to them as if the fighting had gone on forever, for already it had lasted over thirty years.

Now, with Glyn Dŵr's rebellion under control, Henry V was ready to take up the fight once more. This war would be remembered as the Hundred Years War. In the end the King of England, with his English and Welsh soldiers, was completely defeated and forced to leave France to the French people.

Old Ways and New Horizons

Heraldry

Does your school have its own school uniform, with a special badge and motto? Badges and mottos are used to distinguish between different schools and to mark you out as a pupil at a particular school in a particular area. If you study the badge carefully, you will probably learn something about the history of your town or village.

The custom of wearing special badges goes back over nine hundred years in England and Wales. It seems to have developed because Norman knights wore very heavy armour in battle. They covered their horses with drapes, their own bodies with coats of armour, and their heads with strong helmets. On a battlefield it was almost impossible to know who was who, or to tell who was your enemy and who was on your side. Just imagine the confusion and disorder!

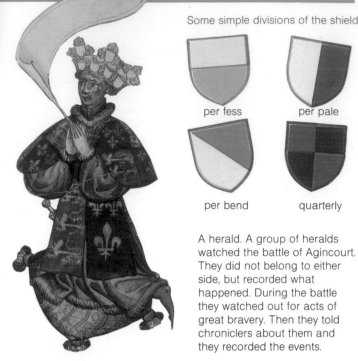

Some simple divisions of the shield

per fess   per pale

per bend   quarterly

A herald. A group of heralds watched the battle of Agincourt. They did not belong to either side, but recorded what happened. During the battle they watched out for acts of great bravery. Then they told chroniclers about them and they recorded the events.

To overcome this problem knights began to carry personal badges, or coats of arms, on their shields, on the pennons or banners on their lances, on their surcoats and on their horses' coverings. Now their own band of soldiers would be able to identify them even in the middle of a fierce battle. In the same way, the soldiers began to wear their lord's arms, so that they could recognize one another. This custom of wearing coats of arms spread quickly throughout Europe in the twelfth century.

The knights also wore their arms in times of peace, especially in the great tournaments which became so popular with the Normans. These tournaments seem to us, nowadays, to be very colourful and glamorous. We've all seen pictures and films of galloping horses, clashing armour and romantic knights giving favours to their chosen maidens. In fact medieval tournaments could be cruel and dangerous events. They attracted wild young men whose aim was to win the horses and armour of the knights they defeated, rather than to behave like gentlemen in a chivalrous fight. We know that Edward I celebrated his great victory over Prince Llywelyn the Last in 1282-3 with a splendid royal tournament at Nefyn in Gwynedd.

A tournament

Some heraldic devices

chevron

saltire

Lord Rhys
ap Gruffudd

Prince Llywelyn
the Great

William de Barry

Sir Rhys
ap Thomas

Sir Hywel of
the Battleaxe

unicorn 'rampant'   eagle 'displayed'

Only noblemen were allowed to own coats of arms. This privilege was guarded jealously and handed down from father to son. To prevent other families stealing coats of arms, heralds were appointed. They had to learn all the different coats of arms and understand their meanings.

A nobleman could design his own coat of arms. At first, the designs were quite simple with perhaps a shield in two colours, divided into quarters. Gradually, as they became more popular, they also became more complicated. Animals, fish, birds and flowers were added, and mythical animals such as dragons, griffins and unicorns were used. According to an essay on coats of arms, written perhaps by a Welshman called Sion Trefor around 1400, each animal had a symbolic meaning. He says that:

'To wear a lion in your coat of arms is a sign of bravery, cruelty, strength, nobility and generosity. A deer is a sign that the bearer was poor in his youth but has become wealthy, he is also wise in battle. A boar stands for a strong, cruel and jealous warrior who would rather die than run away from battle. A swan stands for a good singer. A horse suits a willing . . . and graceful man'.

It is hardly surprising that the main princes of Gwynedd chose to have lions, for bravery and nobility, on their coats of arms. Prince Llywelyn the Great's shield was divided into quarters, with a walking lion, or lion 'passant' according to the French heraldic term, on each quarter. The lions on Owain Glyn Dŵr's shield were even fiercer, as they stood on one hind leg and were called lions 'rampant'. The royal house of Dinefwr in South Wales, on the other hand, chose ravens for its coat of arms.

Unfortunately we don't have pictures of many of these shields, and we have to depend on heraldic descriptions or on the words of poets such as Iolo Goch. In his poem to praise the great soldier Sir Hywel of the Battleaxe, who fought in the French wars of the fourteenth century, Iolo tells us that Sir Hywel carried a black banner with three fleurs-de-lis on it, or as he says:

three pretty white flowers
Of the same shape, with silver leaves.

Anyone can invent his or her own coat of arms. Wales still has its own Welsh Herald Extraordinary, whose work it is to keep an eye on all the registered coats of arms. Even banks, rugby clubs and universities have their own coats of arms today.

Coats of arms of Dyfed County Council (*left*)

and the University of Wales (*right*)

6

A Golden Age for Poets

It is two o'clock on the first Thursday in August, and we've come on a day trip to the National Eisteddfod of Wales. The field is packed with people and we join a queue trying to get into the main pavilion. What are we all going to see?

'I wonder who's won this year', says a gentleman next to us in the queue.

'*Won what?*', we ask in bewilderment.

'Why, the chair of course,' he answers. 'Oh! I see, you're strangers to the Eisteddfod. Well, you're about to witness one of the most important events in the Welsh calendar, the chairing of the bard. The Welsh people are so proud of their special way of writing poetry in *cynghanedd* that they hold a ceremony every year, on Thursday at the Eisteddfod, to honour the best poet. We'd better move on or we'll lose our place.'

As we press forward into the main pavilion, something strange happens, We feel we're going back over five hundred years, to a much earlier Eisteddfod held at Carmarthen in about 1451. It is very different from the National Eisteddfod today. There is no field or main pavilion, but there are music and poetry competitions. The men from Tegeingl, Clwyd, seem to have swept the board. They have won the silver harp for the best harpist, the silver tongue for the best singer and the silver chair for the best bard.

We're lucky enough to have a chance to congratulate Dafydd ab Edmwnd, the winning bard, on his success.

'Thank you', he answers modestly. 'Yes, this Eisteddfod has been an important event. You see, during the great Glyn Dŵr rebellion, poets were punished severely for helping the Welsh prince. They were called wasters and

The chairing of the Bard at a modern National Eisteddfod

tramps, and told that they could no longer wander around the countryside looking for patrons. We bards have decided we must change this. We've come together to improve our craft and to make sure that only trained poets with licences travel the countryside calling themselves bards. New poets have to serve as apprentices, learning their craft for up to nine years, and of course they have to know all the strict rules of *cynghanedd*.'

'*Cynghanedd, mm ... we've heard of that before. What is it?*' we ask.

'It's a complicated system of rules for writing Welsh poetry,' Dafydd explains. 'We have to match up consonants or rhymes, or sometimes both, in one line of poetry,' he laughs. 'There are four different types of *cynghanedd*. If I recite four famous lines of poetry, perhaps you can spot the *cynghanedd* in them. The first two lines come from a sad poem by Lewis Glyn Cothi, to mourn the death of his young son. Listen carefully for the rhymes and matching consonants:

> Yn iach *wên* ar fy *ngen*au
> (Farewell to a smile on my lips)
> Yn iach chwerth*in* o'r m*in* mau
>   m   m
> (Farewell to laughter from my mouth).

And now for something completely different, lines to describe the warm welcome poet Dafydd Nanmor had at a nobleman's home in Dyfed. You can hear the consonants cracking:

Llety a gefais ger llaw teg afon
ll t   g f /   ll   t g f
(I had a place to stay near a fair river)

Llawn o ddaioni a llawen ddynion
ll   n   dd   n / ll   n dd n
(Full of goodness and merry men)'.

As Dafydd ab Edmund speaks, we marvel at the skill of the poets who were able to write fine poems under such strict and difficult rules. No wonder the fifteenth century was considered a golden age for Welsh poets, an age when noblemen, bishops and abbots were proud to welcome bards into their homes and to reward them with gifts of clothes and money for their poems.

In return for this hospitality the bards praised their patrons the noblemen, describing their way of life, and especially what they ate and drank at their grand feasts. Through the poems we see the tables laid with white tablecloths and silver and pewter plates. Three courses were served at every main meal, and in each course there was a choice of seven to twenty dishes, often a strange mixture of sweet and savoury. Many of the meats are unfamiliar to us today, for as well as beef, they ate venison, rabbit, swan, bittern and curlew. The food was well-seasoned with herbs such as sage and thyme, or with spices such as cinnamon, mace, ginger and cloves. Fruits like oranges, apples, pomegranates and grapes added a sweet touch. All this was washed down with plenty of beer, mead, spirits and wines from Burgundy and Spain.

The bards were also like the newspapers of their age, travelling from place to place, carrying news of births, marriages and deaths, singing songs of love, foretelling the future and reporting on plagues, battles and wars. They held as warm a place in Welsh people's hearts then as they do at the National Eisteddfod today.

Henry Tudor – King of England and Wales

Henry Tudor
(Henry VII)

On 22 August 1485, Henry Tudor and his army fought against King Richard III of England and his men at the battle of Bosworth Field. Richard was defeated and Henry was declared King Henry VII of England and Wales. He claimed that as he was part Welsh and part English, he had a right to be king of both countries. The people of England and Wales accepted him as their king and a new stage in history, the Tudor period, began. Who was this Henry Tudor, and how important was his Welsh blood in helping him to become king?

We must begin our story with his grandfather Owen Tudor, one of the most romantic figures in Welsh history. Owen's family claimed that they were descended from Cadwaladr, the last King of the Britons, back in the seventh century. Owen's father had helped Glyn Dŵr in his great rebellion against the English Crown. When the revolt failed, Owen

Tudor of Penmynydd, Anglesey, set out on the greatest adventure of his young life. He was to be a page at King Henry V's court in London.

King Henry V was married to Catherine de Valois, the daughter of the King of France, but by the time she was twenty-two years old Henry had died and left her a young widow. According to one story Owen Tudor caught the Queen's eye when he was out bathing naked one day. He seems to have been a very handsome and clever man because one writer, Polydore Vergil, describes him as being 'adorned with wonderful gifts of body and mind'. Owen and Catherine fell in love and soon they were secretly married. Now Owen was the father-in-law of the young King Henry VI. His own two sons, Edmund and Jasper, were to play an important part in the troubled events of the fifteenth century.

The eldest son, Edmund, became the Earl of Richmond and married Margaret Beaufort. This was a clever move because Margaret could claim to have a right to the throne of England. She was only a young girl at the time of her marriage, but when Edmund died within a year she found she was expecting a baby. In January 1457, in a small room at Pembroke Castle, Margaret gave birth to a baby son, Henry Tudor, the future King of England and Wales. Because his mother was only fourteen years old, Henry's uncle Jasper took him into his care and brought him up in South Wales.

During the next twenty-five years, two noble families claimed the English throne. One was the House of Lancaster, whose badge was a red rose. The other was the House of York, whose symbol was a white rose. The quarrel between these two houses became bitter and developed into a series of battles called 'The Wars of the Roses'.

Because of his sister-in-law Margaret's connections, Jasper fought on the Lancastrian side, and travelled to and fro between Wales and France helping the Lancastrian cause. After one battle in 1461 his father, Owen Tudor, was captured by the enemy and brought to Hereford as a prisoner. Let's join the chronicler William Gregory in the crowded market place at Hereford, to find out what happened to this famous prisoner, the husband of the former Queen Catherine of England.

The barbican gate of Pembroke Castle

There is a strange hush over the market place, which has been prepared for a beheading. The axe and block of wood are ready, but Owen does not seem to understand what is going to happen to him. He feels sure that since he is such an important prisoner, he will be pardoned and set free. But then one of the soldiers rips off the collar of his red doublet. His neck is bare, and suddenly Owen realises that he will not escape the axe. He turns to the crowd and says quietly, 'The head which you are going to put on the stock used to be on Queen Catherine's lap'. Then he turns and bravely goes to his death. The axe falls, and Owen's handsome head is lifted up and placed for all to see on top of the market cross. Poor Owen Tudor's eventful life had ended in a tragic way.

Tomb of Edmund Tudor at
St Davids Cathedral

Frieze showing the Battle of Bosworth, Richard III is on the ground clutching his crown while
Henry Tudor towers over him on horseback

Jasper carried on his fight for the House of Lancaster bravely. Ten years later, when the House of York took the English throne, he and his nephew Henry were forced to flee to Brittany for shelter. The young prince spent the next fourteen years of his life there. Yet, the House of Lancaster still saw him as the main heir to the English throne, and there were many people plotting on his behalf in England.

In Wales, Henry's cause was championed by the poets. As they travelled around the country, they spread news about him and won him more and more support. They were determined to see a Welshman as King of England, and they compared Henry with the great King Arthur who was said to be asleep in a cave in Wales. They believed that King Arthur would return one day to save his people.

Of course the poets couldn't say all these things openly, in case the King of England called them traitors. So they hid the true meaning of their poetry by calling different people different animals. When they mention an ox they usually mean Jasper Tudor; King Richard III is sometimes a raven, a wild boar or a mole; Owen Tudor is a swallow; and Henry himself is called a young bull or an

eagle. Can you understand the references in these lines by Robin Ddu?

> Though the swallow has been beheaded
> There is a great eagle to follow him.

Or these, by the same bard?

> Now the time is upon us
> For the young bull to venture out
>   into the world
> The mole will fall in a civilised way,
> And there will be revenge throughout
>   the land.

Over fifty Welsh poets wrote a total of two hundred poems to foretell the future of Wales. Although many of these poems are deliberately difficult to understand, there can be no doubt that their propaganda persuaded the people of Wales to support a prince of Welsh blood.

By 1485 the time was ripe for Henry to claim the throne of the Britons as King of England and Wales. It isn't surprising that he decided to launch his invasion through Wales, but as he landed at Dale in his native Pembrokeshire with a 'rabble' army of 2,000 foreigners, he must have worried whether the Welsh would help him or not.

Henry was particularly concerned about how the great Lord of Dinefwr, Rhys ap Thomas, would react. One story tells us that Rhys had promised King Richard that he would never allow Henry to cross through his lands except over his body. According to the story Rhys got out of his promise by hiding under a bridge and allowing Henry and his troops to march over it, and so over his body. Unfortunately we have no proof that this ever happened. We do know, however, that Rhys did not support Henry immediately. He followed Henry up into mid-Wales, before eventually deciding to join him in his cause.

Henry did not march eastwards through Wales towards England. Instead he moved north, to mid-Wales, gathering men and arms as he went. On his journey he stayed at the home of the famous poet, Dafydd Llwyd, at Mathafarn, Powys. This poet had spent his life praising Henry Tudor and calling upon him to return, to claim his birthright.

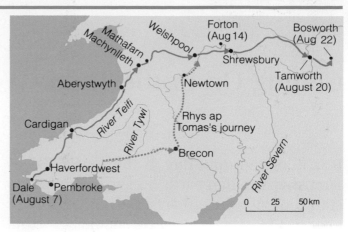

The Way to Bosworth

Mathafarn, Powys, the home of Dafydd Llwyd

A legend says that during his stay, Henry asked Dafydd to foretell whether he would win the battle against King Richard. Poor Dafydd didn't know what to reply. As he tossed and turned in bed that night his wife, claims the story, advised him cleverly. She said, 'Tell Henry that he is sure to win. If he does happen to lose the battle he won't return this way to trouble us, but if he wins you might be well rewarded'. Once more we cannot be sure whether this story is true, but it seems likely that Henry would have asked the advice of his staunchest bardic supporter as he prepared for the greatest day of his life.

Henry Tudor and his army marched to meet Richard and his troops at Bosworth Field near Tamworth in England. Poor Henry didn't seem to have much of a chance. His army was outnumbered by two to one, but at the last moment two powerful brothers from the Stanley family decided to bring their 3,000 soldiers to fight for him. King Richard was defeated and killed on the battlefield. His body was taken, 'naked of all clothing and laid upon the back of a horse with the arms and legs hanging down on both sides' to be buried at Leicester.

The Welsh were overjoyed at Henry's success. As the ambassador for Venice commented, 'The Welsh may be said to have recovered their former independence, for the wise and fortunate Henry VII is a Welshman'. At last a king of Welsh blood had won the crown of Britain and now ruled over both England and Wales. He had avenged all the defeats the Welsh had suffered under Llywelyn the Last and Owain Glyn Dŵr. Surely, the people told one another, King Henry would set them free of the cruel laws which had punished them for being Welshmen? Surely he would reward them with land and jobs for supporting him in his fight? The bards felt that their dreams had come true. 'There is hope for our nation', said one poet, and Dafydd Llwyd himself proclaimed that:

The world is much better for the
    killing of little Richard.
Henry was, will be, and now is.
    Long may he live.

93

Getting On in the Tudor World

It is a fine autumn day in the year 1500 as Sion Llwyd ab Ifan packs his few belongings to start out on the greatest adventure of his young life. He is leaving home in rural Merionethshire and going to London to seek fame and fortune. He'll travel there with the drovers and their cattle, and they're almost ready to set out. Sion seems so excited that it is difficult to persuade him to chat to us before he leaves.

'I can't wait to get to London,' he says. 'It's the only place for an ambitious Welshman these days. Ever since Henry Tudor became King, Welshmen have flocked to England and have got on well in business, as servants in the royal court, and as members of the King's personal bodyguard. King Henry VII has a soft spot for his countrymen, I think.'

'*So the dream of having a Welshman on the throne of England had come true?*' we ask.

'Yes indeed,' replies Sion enthusiastically. 'I've heard that King Henry is very proud of his Welsh blood. He's appointed a group of experts to draw up his family tree, to prove that he's descended from the Welsh princes. He's called Welsh harpists and poets to his court, and they celebrate St David's Day there every year. And, of course, he's named his eldest son, Arthur, in memory of the great King Arthur of the Britons.'

'*But surely,*' we argue, '*if he's such a good Welshman he should make sure that life in Wales*

Rural Meironeth

London, about 1540

Arthur Prince of Wales

itself gets better, so that young men like you don't have to move to London to get on in the world.'

Sion looks a little taken aback. 'He did try, I suppose,' he answers timidly. 'When he became King in 1485 he gave many of those who helped him in battle good jobs in Wales. Do you remember Rhys ap Thomas, Lord of Dinefwr, who joined Henry on his march to Bosworth? Well, Henry knighted him, called him Sir Rhys, and gave him important posts in South Wales. And, of course, he rewarded his 'dearest uncle' Jasper by creating him Duke of Bedford and putting him in charge of South Wales. Yes, his main supporters seem to have done well ...'

'*What about the ordinary people?*' we prod gently.

'Perhaps things haven't gone quite as we expected in Wales itself,' he admits reluctantly. 'Most Welshmen felt sure that King Henry would get rid of the cruel laws passed during the Glyn Dŵr revolt.'

'*You mean the laws punishing Welshmen for being Welshmen?*'

'Yes, laws preventing Welsh people from buying land in England or in English towns in Wales; laws preventing them from living as burgesses in these towns; laws preventing them from holding important jobs (although some have got round these laws, of course); and all the other punishing laws.'

'*Hasn't Henry Tudor, the 'Welsh' king, done anything to change this?*'

'Not yet. Some poets have criticised him for this; one poem goes as far as to say that:

Jasper and Henry prefer
Men from the North more than our men.

That is why I'm leaving Wales. There isn't much of a future here. The future is in the royal court in London. But I can't stand here talking. I must hurry to join the drovers. It's the only safe way to travel to the great city. Farewell, and if you come to London, look me up. But don't forget,' he adds with a laugh, 'don't ask for Sion Llwyd ab Ifan there. I intend changing my name to John Lloyd or John Bevan as soon as I get there. Goodbye.' He waves his hand and hurries off to join the drovers as they take their cattle to the great London fairs.

Many ambitious fortune-seekers like Sion Llwyd left Wales for England in Tudor times. Many of them also changed their names, so that they sounded more English. Huw ab Owen became Hugh Bowen; ap Hywel became Powell; Ifan Goch became Evan Gough; and Dafydd ap Siencyn became David Jenkins. Can you think of any other examples?

For those who stayed in Wales, the dream of a new Tudor world was not fulfilled for many years. It was not until the last years of his reign that Henry began, in some areas, to free Welshmen from the cruel laws passed in Glyn Dŵr's time. As different parts of Wales were ruled by different laws, there was chaos as criminals fled from one area to another to avoid being punished. According to one nobleman, Sir John Wynn, who could remember his grandfather describing North Wales in Henry Tudor's time, it was a 'wild world (where) every man stood upon his guard and did not go out without preparing and arming himself as if he was going to the battlefield'.

One story claims that as Henry Tudor was dying, he called his heir and ordered him 'to have a care for the people of Wales'. Bringing law and order to his father's homeland in Wales would be quite a challenge for the new King, Henry VIII. His answer – an Act of Union to unite England and Wales – would seem to be the final step in the great Norman–English conquest of Wales.

Index